SEEING THE WORLD

PRINCETON STUDIES IN CULTURAL SOCIOLOGY

Paul J. DiMaggio, Michèle Lamont,
Robert J. Wuthnow, and Viviana A. Zelizer,
Series Editors

A list of titles in this series appears at the back of the book.

SEEING THE WORLD

How US Universities Make Knowledge in a Global Era

Mitchell L. Stevens,

Cynthia Miller-Idriss,

and Seteney Shami

Princeton University Press

Princeton and Oxford

Published by Princeton University Press,
41 William Street, Princeton, New Jersey 08540

In the United Kingdom: Princeton University Press,
6 Oxford Street, Woodstock, Oxfordshire OX20 1TR

press.princeton.edu

Jacket art courtesy of Shutterstock

ISBN 978-0-691-15869-3

Library of Congress Control Number: 2017945421

British Library Cataloging-in-Publication Data is available

This book has been composed in Baskerville 10 Pro and Eurostile LT Std

Printed on acid-free paper. ∞

Printed in the United States of America

10 9 8 7 6 5 4 3 2 1

FOR STUDENTS OF PLACES, AND THEIR MENTORS

If you think of a university as sort of like a kaleidoscope—all the pieces—I think the kaleidoscope is turning, as we speak, and the question of what the patterns are going to be when it stops turning is an open one.

—POLITICAL SCIENTIST, SENIOR INTERNATIONAL OFFICER

CONTENTS

ACKNOWLEDGMENTS

Our greatest debt is to the scores of individuals whose words enliven our pages. Despite their busy schedules, the faculty and administrators quoted throughout this book were engaged participants in often lengthy conversations—with strangers. We learned from each of them, and our work simply would not have happened without their contributions.

Nor would it have happened without financial support. Data collection for a pilot project in the field of Middle East studies was funded by the Ford Foundation in 2000 (grant no. 1010–0542). Starting in 2004, with the receipt of funding from the US Department of Education's International Research and Studies Program, the project became a large-scale endeavor focused on Middle East, Russia/Eurasia, South Asia, and Central Asia area studies centers at US universities. The Department of Education provided two successive grants for three phases of data collection and initial analysis through 2010 (grant nos. P017A040075 and P017A060034). A subsequent grant from the Andrew W. Mellon Foundation enabled further data analysis through 2014 (grant no. 31300136).

The Social Science Research Council (SSRC) has been this project's home since 2000. That has meant a great deal. The SSRC was central to the evolution of regionally focused social science in the twentieth century and continues to sustain a commitment to cosmopolitan scholarship. The vision and critical encouragement of SSRC presidents Craig Calhoun and Ira Katznelson have been invaluable to us. Marcial Godoy-Anativia, Nicolas Guilhot, and Srirupa Roy provided a critical overview of the *longue durée* of debates surrounding area studies.

Nazli Parvizi helped conduct data collection for the pilot study; Mary Ann Riad helped us obtain the first US Department of Education grant; and Maureen Abdelsayad coordinated the first major phase of fieldwork. Holly Danzeisen ably managed the second and third phases of fieldwork and held us all together during the many years we took to think it all through. For her patience, and our collective sanity, we thank Holly especially.

Lisa Wedeen, Reşat Kasaba, and Karen Pfeifer served as steering committee members for the newly expanded project from 2004 to 2006, helping conceptualize the research and provide guidance throughout its first phase. Charles Kurzman helped us understand the potential of our inquiry for various audiences over many years.

Our thinking was informed by several SSRC-sponsored consultation meetings at the Middle East Studies Association (MESA 2000, 2003); panels at the first World Congress of Middle East Studies (WOCMES 2002) and the American Sociological Association (ASA 2011); and invited talks at Boston University, UC–Berkeley, and UC–Davis. The SSRC held additional consultation meetings throughout the project's tenure to present empirical research findings as they emerged. In addition to the project's steering committee members, SSRC staff members, and project researchers, attendees at the workshop in 2007 included Lisa Anderson, Laura Bier, Hoda Elsadda, Dmitry Gorenburg, Mervat Hatem, Sangeeta Kamat, David Ludden, Zachary Lockman, Amy Newhall, David Nugent, Jennifer Olmsted, Morton Valbjørn, and Ulrich Wurzel. These discussions shaped thinking about knowledge production on world regions internationally, the dynamic relationship between area studies and disciplines, and the impact of 9/11 on regional inquiry.

We thank these attendees at a 2008 consultation: Jeremy Adelman, Sada Aksartova, Selma Botman, Diana Deborah Davis, J. Nicholas Entrikin, David Frank, Linda Costigan Lederman, Michèle Lamont, Vasuki Nesiah, Jeffrey Riedinger, Gideon Rose, Nancy Ruther, and George Steinmetz. A final 2009 consultation included Thomas Bender, David Engerman, Carl Ernst, Robert Glew, Kathleen Hall, Jerry Jacobs, Aly Kassam-Remtualla, Joe Miesel, Jennifer Olmsted, Nancy Ruther, Toby Alice Volkman, and Steven Wheatley.

A writing workshop at American University in 2014 included Ethan Hutt, Ashley Mears, and Celine-Marie Pascale, who read early chapter drafts and provided incisive feedback. Michèle Lamont and Christopher Loss humored us with innumerable conversations. Two officially anonymous reviewers for Princeton University Press provided serial comment on full versions of the manuscript.

We owe a great deal to the project's researchers, who, supervised by Cynthia Miller-Idriss, undertook the bulk of data collection and coding in three separate phases from 2005 to 2007: Elizabeth Anderson Worden, Nick Gozik, and Anthony Koliha. All of them devoted weeks to campus visits while balancing the demands of their dissertations and other professional commitments. Jeremy Browne played a key role in unlocking the US Department of Education EELIAS/IRIS database and informing the overall methodological architecture of the endeavor. Thanks also go to our other researchers, including Lucine Taminian, who conducted the pilot research survey. Alice Horner performed critical background research and compiled an impressive bibliography. Additional research assistance, much of it funded through New York University's Steinhardt School, was provided by doctoral students Jennifer Auerbach, Christian Bracho, Shane Minkin, Naomi Moland, and Nina Pessin-Whedbee. Stanford doctoral student Jesse Foster contributed meticulous data cleaning and coding support.

Special thanks go to Jonathan Friedman, who, in addition to providing research assistance over the past eight years, served as the project's data manager from 2013 to 2017. In this role Jon assumed the daunting task of making all project evidence interoperable, synthesizing the work of many involved in the project before him and ensuring consistency and accuracy of data presentation.

Mitchell Stevens is additionally grateful to several parties at Stanford University. The Graduate School of Education provided a sabbatical and course release that made it possible to complete the first full book manuscript and its substantial revision. The Institute for Research in the Social Sciences (IRiSS) gave him a physical site for the writing and idyllic working conditions. The Scandinavian Consortium for Organizational Research (SCANCOR) hosted innumerable conversations about this work, and a living case study in a novel means of scaffolding cosmopolitan social science. Many Stanford colleagues lent vision, encouragement, and practical advice: Karen Cook, Tom Ehrlich, Mark Granovetter, Aishwary Kumar, David Labaree, Harry Makler, Dan McFarland, John Meyer, David Palumbo-Liu, Woody Powell, Chiqui Ramirez, Gabriella Safran, Dick Scott, Parna Sengupta, Sarah Soule, Robert Wessling, Kären Wiggen, John Willinsky, and Xueguang Zhou. Niecolle Felix administered finances and proofread with aplomb. Beyond Stanford, Elizabeth Armstrong, Elisabeth Clemens, Carol Heimer, Jerry Jacobs and Jason Owen-Smith have been dedicated thought partners. And whether in New York, Minneapolis, or Palo Alto, Arik Lifschitz has enabled this work with his inimitable, patient wisdom.

Cynthia Miller-Idriss is indebted to New York University (NYU) for sabbatical time in 2011–12, to American University (AU) for leave in 2013–14, and to the Morphomata Center for Advanced Studies at the University of Cologne for a residential fellowship in 2013– 14, which provided essential time for data analysis and writing of early chapter drafts. Several individuals hosted talks and provided feedback on chapter drafts and ideas in critical ways, and she is especially grateful to Tamar Breslauer, Kevin Hovland, Michael Kennedy, Michael Kirst, David Labaree, Chris Loss, Pat McGuinn, Justin Powell, Daniel Tröhler, Bernhard Streitwieser, and Elizabeth Worden for their substantive feedback. Intellectual and collegial support from NYU and AU colleagues Richard Arum, Kim Blankenship, Christian Bracho, Dana Burde, Cheryl Holcomb-McCoy, Sarah Irvine Belson, Peter Starr, Gay Young, and Jon Zimmerman was invaluable. Although all three coauthors were living in New York at the start of this project, by the end we were dispersed across time and space, living in Palo Alto; Washington, DC; and Beirut, with research assistants and project coordinators still based in New York and Brooklyn at NYU and SSRC. Our regular meetings for writing workshops and discussions were subsidized by adding a day or two to related meetings and talks; for this we are indebted to American University's School of Education Global Education Forum, Stanford's Graduate School of Education, and the Social Science Research Council. And finally, Shamil, Aniset, and Nura Idriss' unflagging support from home sustained the project and Cynthia's role in it in unmeasurable ways.

All three of us enjoyed the incomparable professionalism of the editorial and production teams at Princeton University Press. Eric Schwartz signed the project at what would prove to be an earlier stage in its evolution than any of us imagined. Meagan Levinson inherited the effort when it was still substantially hypothetical. She believed, enabled, and saw it through nevertheless. Jenny Wolkowicki deftly shepherded the manuscript through production. And we couldn't ask for a more privileged home for this book than Princeton Studies in Cultural Sociology.

Portions of Chapter 5, "Numbers and Languages," appeared previously in Cynthia Miller-Idriss and Seteney Shami, "Graduate Student Training and the Reluctant Internationalism of Social Science in the USA," *Research in Comparative and International Education* 7(2012):50–60, and are reprinted here by permission of SAGE Publications, Ltd.

Any errors or omissions herein are fully the responsibility of its named authors, but any praise for it will be widely shared.

SEEING THE WORLD

Seeing through the Academy

This book has three primary aims. The first is to offer insight into the mechanics of knowledge production at the arts-and-sciences cores of US research universities. Scholarly understanding of how universities transform money and intellect into knowledge remains limited. At present we have only rudimentary measures of knowledge production's inputs: tuition and fees, government subsidies, philanthropic gifts, and the academic credentials of students and faculty. Output measures are equally coarse: counts of degrees conferred; dissertations, articles, and books completed; patents secured; dollars returned on particular inventions. As for the black box of knowledge production in between: very little. Scholars have only recently made serious attempts to specify and quantify all the components that knowledge production at any great university daily entails: the myriad conversations among students and faculty, the workshops and seminars and working lunches, the chance meetings and office-door gossip sessions, the daily grinds of reading and reviewing and grading that somehow sum to publishable ideas and the occasional history-shaping insight. Basic questions about academic knowledge production remain open. How do universities absorb information from their human inputs and their larger environments? Does academic innovation have a general alchemy or does it vary qualitatively across knowledge domains? How is the knowledge work at the core of universities linked with patron preferences and world affairs? This book offers novel insight into how such questions can be asked and answered.

The second aim is to contribute to the understanding of universities as special mechanisms for seeing the world. Scholars have long recognized that universities are ideal sites to observe social change. The pace of racial integration and the dynamics of gender and sexual relations are examples of important social processes that are both refracted and more clearly understood through their expression in higher education. How universities organize knowledge about the rest of the world also offers important lessons. Institutes on "oriental" civilizations, research projects grounded in modernization theory, study abroad programs offered at particular sites in particular ways— all of these can be leveraged for insight into how academics and their patrons make sense of the world and their changing relation to it across generations.

The third aim is to forward a theory of how US universities themselves change. Universities are peculiar organizations in that they look backward and forward simultaneously. By going to work in lovely old buildings, donning medieval gowns on summer feast days, and issuing paper diplomas written in dead languages, university leaders rehearse their fealty to valued pasts. Yet these same people also are forever building for the future. They continually renovate their academic homes as knowledge grows, as technologies for producing and consuming knowledge evolve, and as the parties that pay for it all shift their predilections and priorities. The largest purpose of this book is to paint a picture of how US research universities manage to reorganize themselves continually while retaining stable identities over time.

Seeing the World is an empirical investigation of the organization of programs devoted to the study of world regions, particularly the Middle East and its neighboring geographies, on US research university campuses in the years following 9/11. It emerges out of a long process of thinking and consultations at the Social Science Research Council (SSRC). Starting in the mid-1990s, the SSRC began reconsidering its international programs in light of the end of the Cold War and accumulating intellectual critiques of the area studies model. In 2000 the SSRC received a small grant from the Ford Foundation to rethink the Program on the Middle East and North Africa, specifically. The 9/11 attacks gave the initiative urgency, not least because of public and political polemic directed at Middle East studies programs. Momentum was brought to the initiative by a 2003 call for proposals issued by the US Department of Education's Office of Postsecondary Education International Research and Studies Program, which specifically sought research to "improve and strengthen instruction in modern foreign languages, area studies, and other international fields." The call prioritized "Studies assessing the outcomes and effectiveness of programs authorized under Title VI of the Higher Education Act of 1965," as well as work focused on "the Middle East, Central Asia, and South Asia."[1]

First among us to respond to that call was Seteney Shami, who at the time was heading the Middle East and Russia/Eurasia portfolios of SSRC. Her original proposal to the Department of Education focused on Middle East Studies regarding three challenges facing the field: a paradigmatic one, posed by the advancement of global integration and the rise of the globalization paradigm; a disciplinary one, marked by ongoing scholarly debate about the value of contextual knowledge in the social sciences and a seeming withdrawal of economists, political scientists, and sociologists from regionally focused scholarship; and a public one in the post-9/11 period, which had increased the workload of centers and created "a sense of heightened responsibility and accountability."[2]

Shami found an ideal lead researcher in Cynthia Miller-Idriss, a sociologist and ethnographer then at New York University, who had developed expertise in various scholarly literatures on nationalism and identity to inform her study of right-wing extremism in post-reunification Germany.[3] Miller-Idriss designed a qualitative-comparative strategy for investigating how universities receiving Title VI grants organize regional scholarship.

The project's earliest questions focused on how area studies centers were responding to increasingly prominent calls for interdisciplinarity and globalization in the US academy. Shami and Miller-Idriss were aware that area studies programs were peopled more heavily by historians and humanists than disciplinary social scientists. They wanted to understand why area studies centers had not generated more inquiries on contemporary political, social, cultural, and economic developments in their target regions. They also wanted to know how area studies programs were finding their niches while administrators' embrace of the "global" idea was rapidly accelerating.

SSRC's founding role in area studies and the imprimatur of Title VI funding brought privileged access to many articulate lights in the American academic firmament. From 2005 to 2009 Shami and Miller-Idriss oversaw the work of a team of SSRC staff researchers, doctoral students, and consulting faculty to build interview, survey, and focus group instruments; finalize site selection; specify interview respondents; conduct site visits; gather data from Department of Education archives; transcribe audio recordings and field notes; and conduct preliminary analyses of incoming evidence.

By the time data collection was coming to a close, the team recognized its potential to inform conversations about the US academy well beyond the domain of area studies. For this they enlisted Mitchell Stevens to join the effort. Having just finished an organizational ethnography of selective college admissions and a critical review of higher education scholarship in the social sciences, Stevens brought complementary expertise.[4] Together we came to view this project as an opportunity to specify the organizational mechanics linking patrons' priorities with the core academic business of US higher education. Together we developed the analytic strategy and data coding scheme that enabled us to find our way to the argument here. More broadly, the project has produced numerous outputs in the form of internal reports and white papers, articles in peer-reviewed journals, and book manuscripts.[5] The first part of the project, focusing on Middle East studies, culminated in a volume edited by Shami and Miller-Idriss entitled *Middle East Studies for the New Millennium: Infrastructures of Knowledge*.[6] As the writing that would become *Seeing the World* developed ever further into an inquiry about higher education and organizational change, Stevens assumed lead authorship.

From the wealth and variety of evidence assembled for the larger SSRC inquiry, this book relies largely on interviews with faculty and administrators at eight of the project's twelve research universities. We limited our scope of inquiry here to these eight schools because we had highly similar interview samples from each of them. These eight include both public and private universities, either of moderate or very large size relative to the organizational population, and they are located throughout the continental United States. All of them are highly regarded research institutions with multiple centers funded by Title VI. At each of the eight schools, we interviewed the following:

Area studies center directors. These positions are typically held as additional appointments by faculty whose primary, tenured appointments are in a disciplinary department of humanities or social sciences.

Area studies center associate directors. These positions are typically defined as administrative appointments and are occupied by staff who hold an advanced degree (often but not always the PhD) in a field of study somehow related to the region. These are the people who maintain day-to-day center activities. Their duties include scheduling courses, managing master's programs, maintaining websites, hosting events and visitors, writing grant proposals, and administering funds for travel and language training that are hallmark assets of Title VI programs.

Chairs of disciplinary departments of economics, political science, and sociology. Because our project had always been focused on the place of the social sciences in regional inquiry, we specifically sought the perspective of these senior leaders of disciplinary programs.

Deans or vice provosts of international/global affairs. Five of our eight case universities had high-level administrative appointees charged with encouraging and coordinating international activity. These interviews enabled us to get a sense of how university leaders were envisioning their schools' relationships with the rest of the world more broadly.

Various members of our team investigated the field evidence collected through the site visits as well as a large stock of archival material, all of which has influenced our thinking. We limit our analysis here to transcribed interviews—seventy-three in number, with a total of eighty people—partly to constrain the cacophony that accompanies any large qualitative inquiry. But we also wanted to make fullest use of the great richness of the interview material. Our respondents make their livings making sense of complicated things. As scholars they are trained to find order in piles of numerical data, immense archives, and long historical traditions. As administrators they survive and flourish in labyrinthine university bureaucracies. And because they are steeped in a wide variety of intellectual fields, they often see the world quite differently from one another. Many of our respondents had invested a great deal of their professional lives navigating the scholarly and organizational terrains of our investigation, and they had a lot to say. We try to honor that fact in these pages by letting their often witty, occasionally angry, and consistently thoughtful insights have their day.

Interviews were almost always conducted face to face, on site at a location of the respondents' choosing, usually in their offices.[7] We asked center directors and associate directors to talk about their units' organizational structure and mission and geographic and thematic scope. We also asked about their specific relationships with university central administration and with disciplinary departments and schools across campus. Through these conversations we tried to understand center autonomy around finances, staffing, curriculum, and student enrollments as well as major constraints on autonomy. We asked social science department chairs to explain whether and how graduate students balanced disciplinary training with regional specialization, and what kinds of resources were available for those who wished to do so. We asked senior international officers about changes in campus climate and culture around the idea of "the global" in recent years and whether those changes had any impact on centers.

The interviews were audio-recorded and transcribed verbatim. Participation in the study was voluntary and we promised both individual and institutional anonymity to respondents. Although none of the authors conducted interviews themselves (we relied on the great skills of Elizabeth Anderson Worden, Nick Gozik, and Anthony Koliha for that), we came to know the interview material very intimately through multiple rounds of transcription checking and coding that took place from 2011 to 2014. Stanford doctoral student Jesse Foster was part of our team from 2011 to 2013, making substantial contributions to our coding scheme. NYU doctoral student Jon Friedman contributed extensive analytic assistance from 2011 right up to the book's completion. This has been a deeply collective project through and through.

Here is a brief sketch of what follows. Chapter 1 offers a schematic description of the three major ways in which US universities have conceived of the rest of the world throughout their history. Members of the US academy have long held cosmopolitan ambitions, but those have been refracted through very different ways of making sense of others and of the perceived location of the United States in the global order. As US academic planners inscribe successive visions of the world onto universities through practical administrative decisions, they contribute to a complex intramural ecosystem. Fresh capacity is built alongside established units, new functions are layered on top of inherited ones, and universities overall become more complicated mechanisms for producing knowledge as they move through time.

In Chapter 2 we consider the creation of "area studies" as we came to study them as creatures of the Cold War. Area studies were components of the scientific/intellectual movement of modernization theory, whose elite academic progenitors secured steady federal patronage for the production of social knowledge that might inform US foreign policy worldwide. Although the grand ambitions of the modernization project were hardly realized, among its more durable legacies were academic units specifically purposed with the production of applied and/or policy-relevant social knowledge throughout the US academy.

Chapter 3 describes the general organizational architecture for producing knowledge at the arts-and-sciences cores of research universities. The basic design is simple, comprising a binary division of academic units into departments that enjoy tenured faculty appointments, doctoral training programs, and the privilege of self-governance, and not-departments that vary widely in size and form. Not-departments go by many names: *institute, center, program, forum,* and *project* are currently common monikers. The number and variety of not-departments and the ease of creating more of them are the source of much of the organizational complexity and dynamism of US universities.

Chapter 4 details the cooperation routines that bind academic subunits together. On every campus we studied, strong norms about the importance of co-sponsorship enabled departments and not-departments alike to pool resources in pursuit of shared goals. This culture of joint ventures is especially important for not-departments, whose budgets, prestige, and durability are typically more precarious than those of units enjoying department status. The combination of stable departments, flexible not-departments, and widely shared techniques for cooperation between them is central to the knowledge production machinery of US universities.

In Chapter 5 we consider why the nation's discipline-based social scientists so consistently neglect the study of world regions beyond the United States. Here we listen especially closely to academic chairs of economics, political science, and sociology departments, who explain how status rewards accrue much more predictably to doctoral students working on heartland disciplinary problems and to the departments training such students. Because the heartland problems are overwhelmingly defined in the context of countries bordering the northern Atlantic Ocean, discipline-based prestige and hiring processes systematically produce regional parochialism in economics, political science, and sociology.

We conclude by showing how the rise of "global" discourse in the US academy has coevolved with fundamental changes in academic patronage, university prestige systems, and the international political economy. America's great research institutions are now only partly servants of the US nation-state. This fact has very large implications for those who make their careers producing scholarly knowledge.

CHAPTER 1

The World in US Universities

By definition, universities comprise the universe of knowledge, the whole of what is known. This conceit is a challenge for academic managers. Deciding how the whole of knowledge should be approximated, and how specialist scholars should be chosen, placed, and put into commerce with one another are fundamental planning tasks for any institution of higher learning.[1] Here we consider one aspect of this conceit: how US universities have refracted knowledge about the rest of the world, over time and into the present. We want to know how universities organize the tasks of making and disseminating scholarship about things beyond US national borders. This chapter provides an overview of three primary ways in which US universities have done this throughout their history.

We also make a novel argument about universities: they are cumulative organizations. They retain things: tenured faculty, functions, programs of study, library and museum collections, and entire means and mechanisms for producing knowledge. This tendency toward retention is exceptional in a contemporary world in which management and therapeutic experts alike preach the virtues of flexibility, downsizing, shedding baggage, and letting go. Universities' predilection for retention continues nevertheless, making them ever more complex organizations as they move through time. The implications of this accumulated complexity for the character of knowledge production and academic careers are among this book's central concerns.

To understand how university leaders and scholars make sense of the rest of the world at different moments in history, we borrow the notion of *schemata* from scholars in cognitive science. Schemata are "knowledge structures that represent objects or events and provide default assumptions about their characteristics, relationships, and entailments under conditions of incomplete information."[2] Like the image on the box of a jigsaw puzzle, a schema enables people to assemble bits of knowledge into a coherent whole. Think of academic inquiries about the rest of the world as an ever-accumulating pile of puzzle pieces. Schemata—sets of preexisting assumptions, ideas, opinions, or principles that may or may not be held consciously—enable academic planners to place those inquiries into more or less coherent intellectual and organizational designs. A schema for making sense of the world provides the default assumptions on which myriad academic decisions are made. They are as often implied as explicitly stated: subtly in evidence when (for examples) faculty and fund-raisers make arguments about what a university "needs" that it doesn't already have; when deans and provosts defend decisions about why particular faculty or endowments "belong" together; or when young scholars plot careers in light of "where the field is going." Schemata simplify otherwise daunting complexity and make it amenable for practical organizational expression at particular places and times.[3]

Three general schemata have informed how academic leaders have conceived of the relationship between their schools and the rest of the world throughout the history of US higher education. The first is a *civilizational* schema that defines schools as repositories of knowledge and artifacts about other places and peoples that can usefully inform the education of young citizens. In this schema the rest of the world is imagined as a discrete number of distinct and bounded cultural, linguistic, and/or ethno-religious traditions. The second is a *national* schema that defines schools as consultants to the US state in its geopolitical ambitions worldwide. In this schema the rest of the world is imagined as a mosaic of nation-states clustered in "areas" of academic and political concern. The third is a *global* schema that defines schools as cosmopolitan agents ecumenical in patronage and borderless in reach. In this schema the rest of the world is imagined as a complex of flows—of people, capital, ideas, goods, and services—often leveraged for university benefit through myriad interorganizational joint ventures.

We refer to all three schemata in the present tense because despite their chronological emergence, no prior one disappears as a subsequent one arises. The schemata and their organizational artifacts accumulate over time, accreting a complicated intramural ecology amenable to the metaphor of a coral reef. Although the introduction of each schema might be marked by pivotal historical events—the founding of the United States, World War II, and the end of the Cold War, respectively—the transitions between schemata are not crisp. Instead universities accumulate schemata and their various organizational expressions over time.

Table 1.1 provides a summary of the arguments we elaborate in subsequent pages.

We recognize that our treatment is written at a great analytic distance. We have neither the space nor the varied expertise required to fully portray the rich historical evolution that is skeletally depicted here. Our goal is to suggest what sociologist Geneviève Zubrzycki has called a "historical sociology of the present:" a critical recognition of features of the past that are implicated in contemporary institutional arrangements.[4]

Table 1.1: Three Schemata for Seeing the World in US Higher Education

	United States in the World	Patrons/ Clients	Knowledge Production about the Rest of the World	Organizational Components
Civilizational	Ambitious nation	Regional elites and philanthropists, state legislatures, civic governments	Civilizations, exotic others, culture areas, and civilizational traditions of presumed coherence	Libraries, museums, civilizational experts, institutes, programs of study, travel
Change drivers: World War II and the Cold War; national ambition to create a virtuous democratic modernity				
National-Service	Superpower in a polarized world	Federal government, foundations	Modernization, science/measurement, security, empowerment; nations and regions presumed to be semi-coherent by politics, language, culture, and geographic contiguity	Areas studies, comparative politics, regional anthropology, social sciences of development, study abroad, international student body
Change drivers: end of the Cold War, global integration of production, chronic budget crises in state higher education, crisis of representation, 9/11				
Global	Anxious superpower in a multipolar world	Foreign governments, corporations, worldwide donors	Pluralism/polyvocality, regions problematic, presumed hybridity, fluidity, complexity, incoherence	Reciprocal agreements, satellite campuses, research partnerships, deans of global programs, commodity service to global clients

Civilizing Others and Ourselves

When we speak of a *civilizational* schema we refer to how American educators in the eighteenth and nineteenth centuries saw the world in terms of coherent historical legacies and geographically contiguous cultural regions. This schema was both a consequence of and a contributor to the intellectual project of imperialism, which imagined modern Europe as an apex of historical evolution and an Archimedean point from which to view the rest of the world.[5] John Willinsky has thoughtfully detailed how nineteenth-century instructional materials of all kinds helped shape Euro-American publics' perceptions of the world as divided into primitive and civilized, or East and West. Museums, gardens, maps, encyclopedias, traveling exhibitions, zoos, and botanical displays served to "educate the eye to divide the world according to the patterns of empire."[6] In their approaches to the rest of the world, American colleges did much the same thing.

This claim may seem paradoxical given the United States' founding antipathy to empire and the regional parochialism of its schools at their founding.[7] Congress declined to mandate Thomas Jefferson's proposal for a national university during the early years of the new republic, leaving the task of higher learning to states and local communities. Americans took up the charge with great enthusiasm. Religious pluralism meant that leaders of every Christian tradition and denomination wanted to build schools to grow their own faiths and train their own successors. Westward expansion brought additional incentives for school founding, as frontier businesspeople and civic leaders built colleges to signal that their places were cosmopolitan destinations, on the make and on the rise. The names of many schools—the Universities of Rochester, Michigan, and California, for example—clearly reflect their founding priority as markers of place.

Yet even while the early colleges were religiously and regionally parochial, their founding missions invariably included the cultural edification of students and local communities. This meant instruction in the lives and wisdom of distant others. Early college leaders and faculty regarded themselves as keepers and teachers of civilizations instantiated in languages, literary and philosophical texts, and artistic artifacts. They organized curricula in languages and history conceived in categorical and epochal terms. Course catalogues and library displays named ancient Roman, Ottoman, and Far Eastern civilizations. Even with the rise of new ideas about science and service to region that coevolved with the land-grant movement around the time of the Civil War, in their regard for the rest of the world US academic leaders maintained core missions as civilizational archivists and civilizing instructors.

Modeled on British and German traditions, curricula in American colleges inherited and perpetuated systems of knowledge categorization that had emerged through European colonialism. Scholarly domains explicitly defined by what Europeans found exotic, such as Oriental studies, Egyptology, and anthropology, fostered ways of thinking about the world as divided into specifiable, bounded cultures. As Michael Kennedy and Miguel Centeno have argued, the idea that distant civilizations had their own cultural logics shaped "the ways in which we recognize similarities and differences, and even envision space and time[.]"[8] The civilizational schema posits civilizations as tangible things. Traces of them can be collected and represented in a local academic organization through expert faculty, library collections, artifact displays, visiting natives, and seasoned travelers.

This schema has proved remarkably durable. It survived even the fundamental reorganization of the US academy into disciplinary departments at the turn of the twentieth century. This process, which we discuss in detail in Chapter 3, entailed the reciprocal development of the undergraduate major and the academic professional associations that would ultimately organize faculty labor markets around topical abstractions. The study of arts and letters came to be organized by departments defined by language, period, and genre. A domain of social inquiry once called "political economy" divided into occupational and intellectual categories of economics, political science, and sociology.[9] While the new social sciences were implicitly and preponderantly about US society, the civilizational schema lived on through departments and various academic units devoted to the study of others: European languages and history; anthropology, archeology, and classics departments; and institutes of Oriental studies. Many of these units have survived into the present.

In the Nation's Service

The nation-state as the primary and presumptive frame for apprehending societies was long in the making. Edward Said, among others, has shown how the building of the nation-state in Europe—in all its facets, from domestic life to economy—was dependent on maintaining empire abroad.[10] After World War II, as the last colonial empires crumbled, the rest of the world began to be described as "new nations" or "developing nations" or "newly independent states." The civilizational schema lost its dominance in US academic life, even while the disciplines and research agendas it had produced continued and even flourished.

For the social sciences, the years immediately following World War II were pivotal. They saw the creation of a new way of organizing regional inquiry that would come to be called *area studies*, and a newly explicit notion of universities as agents of national service. Both phenomena were implicated in the rise of the US (sometimes called the "first new nation"[11]) as the hegemonic world power, as well as the military ascent of the Soviet Union and the emergence of a so-called "third world" as a theatre of Cold War competition.[12] We call this the *national* schema because its champions imagined universities as consultants to the US government and its larger ambitions in the world.[13] Although a few of the most prestigious schools of the nineteenth century had made explicit commitments to national service, mostly in their efforts to create a national leadership class through their undergraduate enrollments, most universities were focused primarily on service to their home regions into and through the world wars.[14] This changed dramatically after 1945. Emboldened by steadily expanding government contracts for research during wartime mobilizations and by the history-making GI Bill, which swelled university classrooms with returning veterans, academics' strategic appreciation for the value of national service steadily grew.[15] Many American academics eagerly embraced new roles as Cold War consultants to the United States in world affairs, and benefited from steady funding from the US military and allied government agencies.[16] Indeed this period is so important for the current fate of social knowledge production on world regions that we devote Chapter 2 to depicting it.

World Wars I and II transformed America's implication in world affairs and encouraged change in how its citizens regarded distant others. Military service and war news from abroad meant that foreign places became significantly more present in the lives of ordinary Americans. For academics, the international became a vast frontier of tantalizing problems whose investigation might be subsidized by government funding. In the wake of scientists' myriad contributions to military endeavors during the wars, federal agencies continued to view universities as vital sources of expert knowledge that could be deployed in service to national security during peacetime and, through the "development" of foreign places, to US national interests all over the world. George Steinmetz notes that "military sources made up the largest share of social science funding from World War II until well into the 1960s."[17] During this period universities became ever more elemental to the "government out of sight" that gave the United States a large and diffuse state apparatus through cooperating social institutions.[18] The federal government would continue to invest heavily in universities for a wide range of defense and diplomacy efforts throughout the subsequent decades.

It was a heady time for academics, one that rewarded faith in the progressive value of applied social science knowledge. Taking advantage of steady government patronage, university leaders eagerly pursued new roles for their institutions in the orchestration of world affairs. Not everyone viewed the strengthening relationship between government and universities positively. The sociologist C. Wright Mills sharply criticized what he viewed as social scientists' irresponsible turn away from scholarly autonomy as they collaborated with clients in government, the military, and the private sector, warning that "if social science is not autonomous, it cannot be a publicly responsible enterprise."[19] The Society for the Study of Social Problems (SSSP) was founded in 1951 with an explicit aim to counter mainstream sociology's shift toward scientism and service to the federal government with an alternative movement that might retain the discipline's critical edge.[20] But many social scientists embraced the turn to national service, signing on as consultants to a wide range of military and governmental agencies and contributing to the growing prestige of quantitative analyses of large national and transnational datasets underwritten by government agencies.[21]

Under the national schema, knowledge about the rest of world has two broad purposes. First, it provides strategic intelligence about specific world regions in service to the US government's national security needs. During the waning years of World War II, academic experts on the Soviet Union had already embraced their new role as what historian David Engerman has called the "professor-consultant," advising Washington elites on foreign policy decisions even as they continued to publish and teach on their home campuses.[22] Their protagonists boasted "that the 'new social sciences' could shape the postwar period as much as atomic physics had shaped the war itself."[23] The onset of the Cold War added urgency to the perceived need for scholarly knowledge on Eastern Europe especially, spurring the federal government and foundations to expand funding to support a national cadre of regional experts. Research agendas, faculty hires, institutes, and programs of study focusing on foreign regions expanded dramatically during the 1950s and '60s.[24]

Second, under the national schema academic expertise is expected to progressively improve the human condition. During the early Cold War this expectation took the form of a scientific/intellectual movement under the banner of modernization theory, what Michael Kennedy and Miguel Centeno have justly called "one of the most remarkably internationalist projects ever."[25] Its purview encompassed both the industrialized "first world" of the United States and Europe and a vast swath of the globe called the "third world," whose problems included food scarcity, poverty, inadequate infrastructure, fragile political institutions, and ethnic conflict. The basic tenet of modernization theory was that given the right inputs any country might eventually develop into a democratic, industrialized, and reasonably prosperous nation-state.[26] With the asserted centrality of capitalist markets, the overall enterprise also entailed pulling new nations away from the Soviet orbit, tightly conjoining political and economic goals. Imagining modernization and development as a linear scale along which societies progressed enabled its American proponents to distinguish their efforts from preceding colonialisms and their assertion of hierarchies between rulers and ruled, while also enabling American academics to place their own nation at a pinnacle of virtuous development.[27] Modernization theory encouraged a view of the United States as the "yardstick against which the achievements and failures of other countries were measured," as Björn Wittrock has put it.[28] "While this was about explaining how other societies might change," write Kennedy and Centeno, "it was also about America itself and its view of the good society."[29] The alignment of several forces—the progress of decolonization, the optimism of twentieth-century social science, chronic vagaries of the Cold War conflict—combined to catapult social scientists' ideas about modernization and development into prominence in the 1950s and 1960s.[30]

Government funding for global intelligence and world influence through the modernization project combined with academics' own ambitions to make US universities centers for official international expertise during the middle of the twentieth century. By housing government-sponsored research, providing guidance to federal agencies, and academic training to future government officials, university leaders could believe that they were serving the progressive interests of the nation and the rest of the world simultaneously. As we will revisit in Chapter 2, this is the context in which federal funding gave birth to the National Defense Education Act of 1958 and thus to area studies centers on US university campuses as we came to study them.

Academic programs funded by government and private foundations that defined third world development as their object of study escalated during the 1960s. So too did criticisms of the foreign policies those programs aimed to serve. Many would note turning points in the Project Camelot scandal, in which a military-sponsored social science project was revealed to have counterinsurgency aims, and in the war in Vietnam.[31] The optimism about academic internationalism in service to nations and their improvement began to fade at the end of the 1960s as quickly as it had arisen after World War II. Social scientists came to recognize that the world's political, economic, and public-health problems were a good deal more complicated than early modernization theory had imagined. The critiques of dependency and world systems theories, both of which posited fundamentally exploitative relations between industrial Europe and North America and the rest of the world, precipitated a deep rethinking of the basic tenets of the modernization idea.[32] Whose modernization was it, and was it everywhere a realizable or even desirable goal? The triumphalism of early Cold War modernization discourse came to share space with critical retrospection and novel theorizations of alternative and multiple modernities.[33]

Yet by then government and foundation moneys had already transformed the study of world regions. Modernization's advocates and critics alike benefited from funding for area studies. Academic careers, instructional and research programs, and whole fields of knowledge developed during this period have endured, even after the rise of a third schema for conceiving relationships between US universities and the rest of the world.

Going Global

When we speak of a *global* schema, we refer to a way of thinking about universities that defines them as hubs and value creators for an internationally cosmopolitan roster of clients and patrons. This accompanies an understanding of the world as increasingly linked through flows of ideas, goods, and people. Although its relative youth obliges us to be tentative in our narration, the global schema appears to have coalesced in the1990s at the conjuncture of four major developments in US academic history: the end of the Cold War; a leveling of government funding for university operations and research; enhanced competition among universities for students, donors, and prestige; and an intellectual revolution in the humanities and humanistic social sciences that undermined the ontological stability of "others." All of these developments exist in a broader context in which digital technologies have dramatically increased the velocity of information exchange and enabled new ways in which geographically distributed academic relationships can be enacted.

It would be difficult to overstate the importance of the end of the twentieth-century Cold War on the dynamics of change in US research universities. This fact has only recently been fully recognized, no doubt in part because today's academics still inhabit the organizational infrastructure built in the Cold War decades of government largesse to higher education. Much of what are currently taken for granted as constitutive features of research universities are outcomes of that past era. Massive basic-research projects funded by the federal government; overhead charges well over 50 percent on federal grants; schools and institutes of international foreign policy; routine exchanges of personnel with federal agencies: all are legacies of the complicated compact between universities and Washington as part of the Cold War. That it was a golden era for US higher education makes its passing all the harder for its beneficiaries to acknowledge. Nevertheless it is true: the steadily rising and unquestioned flow of government resources into universities in the 1950s, '60s, and '70s ended in the subsequent decades and, despite the consternation of many esteemed academic leaders, is not likely soon to resume.[34]

At the same time the federal government was renegotiating its financial relationship with universities for research, state legislatures were rewriting the terms of their support for basic infrastructure and student instruction in public colleges and universities. This was partly a function of what sociologist Isaac Martin has called "the permanent tax revolt": the chronic contraction, in the last decades of the twentieth century, in the willingness of American citizens to pay taxes and in the capacity of state governments to levy them.[35] Other changes have abetted stagnation or erosion in state government support for public higher education. Skyrocketing costs of healthcare and retirement pensions for civil employees, steadily growing prison populations and attendant costs to states for incarceration, an aging baby boom cohort whose own life priorities have changed their exercise of political leverage as voters—all have combined to make funding for higher education a more fungible component of state budgets.[36]

In response, universities have looked ever further afield for new sources of revenue.[37] Abetted by changes in intellectual property law, they have found new ways to partner with private industry to support basic and applied research and to share in the financial returns to proprietary knowledge.[38] Public universities have eagerly courted out-of-state students, charging substantially higher tuition and fees and using the revenues to subsidize other ventures.[39] Public and private universities alike have substantially expanded their recruitment of wealthy foreign nationals, trading on the enduring cachet of American higher education abroad.[40] And they have raised tuition and fees for everyone, contributing to a decades-long and astonishingly steep rise in the cost of four-year residential higher education.[41]

This search for new sources of revenue has encouraged the rise of the global schema. University leaders continue to explain their institutions as servants of their regions and US federal government agencies to the extent that these remain important sources of revenue. But academic fund-raisers hardly limit themselves to regionally or nationally parochial clients. They now actively seek patronage by private companies, foreign governments, and wealthy families worldwide.[42]

A trio of intellectual developments in multiple academic fields further fueled the rise of the global schema. The first posited a qualitative change in the economic forces shaping the global order. Financialization, the growth of transnational corporate firms, spatially distributed industrial production: all were accompanied by modes of governance that went through and beyond the nation-state.[43] The second concerned the status of "others" in North American and European scholarship. Perhaps most prominently exemplified by Edward Said's landmark critique of Eurocentric knowledge, *Orientalism*, since the 1970s scholars in a range of disciplines have pursued careful critiques of how European and North American scholars helped to "other" entire populations and cultural groups even while purporting to discover and describe them. The realization that academic inquiry was implicated in projects of European and American imperialism worldwide precipitated what many humanistic scholars, especially, defined as an intellectual crisis. Many of its proliferating polemics could be boiled down to a single, hard question: what were the political stakes entailed in "us" studying "them"?[44]

Third, scholars throughout the social sciences and humanities were coming to imagine their objects of study as flows and webs rather than static objects. To traditional specializations in Europe, the United States, or Latin America, for example, historians developed a new terrain of study called the "Atlantic world"—a dense network of relationships among reciprocally implicated peoples and places connected by maritime exchange.[45] Subsequent versions of what would come to be called globalization theory advocated for the analytic primacy of the transnational movement of financial capital, human beings, and cultural ideas across the borders of states and regions.[46]

Historical changes influenced the intellectual ones. Just as the mid-twentieth century demise of European colonialism and the creation of new sovereign states encouraged academics to critically reexamine the civilizational schema, the fall of the Berlin Wall in 1989 and the subsequent dissolution of the Soviet Union occasioned fresh debates among political strategists and academics about how "transitions to democracy" would be managed and how global governance of "free" world markets would be organized. Then came 9/11, and much anxiety among academic leaders and government officials about the place and primacy of Middle East inquiry, especially, on US university campuses. Together these phenomena brought into question the founding premises of area studies programs. AIDS, climate change, Facebook, ISIS: all were fateful realities recognizing no single national sovereign or geographic boundary. In this new world, what did it any longer mean to specify a region as an object of inquiry or the nation-state as a primary unit of analysis?[47]

We might summarize the legacies of the three schemata this way. The civilizational schema defines the rest of world as an exotic realm for scholarly inquiry, whose knowledge and artifacts are *collectable* by universities in the form of learned persons and carefully chosen objects. The national schema defines the rest of the world as an array of problems that are potentially *solvable* by systematic, applied academic inquiry. The global schema defines the world as a complex of flows *traversable* by cosmopolitan students and faculty, properly enabled by great universities.

The Coral Reef

In the US academy the civilizational, national, and global schemata are cumulative, not replicative. New ways of thinking about the world and their attendant organizational strategies get layered on top of prior ones, creating a complicated archaeology. This accumulation means that today's universities bear many traces of their pasts even while their leaders build for the future.[48]

One of our colleagues suggested an organic metaphor for this accumulation. Imagine a research university as a coral reef: a composite of organisms at varying stages of development and decay. New life does not fully replace what came before it. Instead the older entities provide scaffold and succor for the younger ones as the entire ecosystem evolves. While hardly the result of any rational planning, the overall entity nevertheless has integrity, coherence, and even beauty as it sustains intellectual lives and livelihoods over time.[49] The area studies centers that are the focus of our inquiry here are vivid examples of how academic organizational forms can endure in this environment. Conceived at a peculiar moment in history, area studies programs nevertheless have remained active components of the intramural ecologies that structure the study of world regions in the US academy.

One senior international officer put it this way:

> [This university] is one of those few institutions that truly spans the globe. It took that Cold War area studies mandate very seriously and established centers and institutes that essentially cover the whole world. So in a funny way we either should be basking in our great success or actually lamenting the fact that we are operating under an old paradigm.

When our interviewer asked what was meant by *old paradigm*, the officer continued in a tone of amused ambivalence:

> Meaning area studies. The Cold War area studies paradigm. I see my mandate as obviously taking the best of what area studies can offer with the obvious caveat that most people who do it don't . . . believe in the over-arching ideology of area studies, first of all because the Cold War ended. That kind of a useful geographical bracketing that was imposed at the time doesn't really seem to apply as well at least in the current world as it turns out. . . . So the upshot is much of what [our unit] is trying to promote is transdisciplinary, trans-area studies.

Traces of the civilizational schema were evident on all the campuses we studied. They were perhaps most vivid in the endurance of courses and programs of study in ancient languages and civilizational history, but they also appeared in the expressed convictions and work practices of area studies personnel. For example, the director of a Russia/Eurasia studies center at a large public university believed that his program had

> . . . a mission in the larger community, and especially our region because indeed we're one of the only post-Soviet [centers] in the South. . . . We are kind of it, really, for the Slavic departments around this part of the country.

He went on:

> I really do view our role as absolutely essential to our students, many of whom believe that the borders of the United States end at El Paso and Amarillo and that's it . . . there is no reason to go anywhere else . . . I am just devoted to the idea that they are going to get at least some information about this part of the world, that covers a sixth of the planet.

Even while he sits in an organizational unit that is a product of the Cold War, this director explains his job partly in terms of an earlier idea of bringing traces of a distant region to his university's own physical environs.

The civilizational schema lives on as well in enduring commitments to collect and display physical artifacts from distant places. In a different, joint interview, this same center director and his associate spoke with pride about an ongoing acquisition project related to central Asia. The director noted that he routinely encouraged faculty traveling in the region to bring objects back home with them:

DIRECTOR: We almost always give them, in addition to the regular travel funds, we'll give them small amounts of money if they agree to pick up bits and pieces of realia that we can then use as part of our outreach travel trunks—our culture kits—so they may bring bits of clothing, bits of souvenir-y type things that we put into our elementary and junior high outreach programs.

ASSOCIATE: Rugs for the yurt . . .

DIRECTOR: Yes, that's right . . .

ASSOCIATE: We now have a yurt . . .

DIRECTOR: . . . we purchased a yurt

ASSOCIATE: . . . on campus and so we're getting cultural bits for the inside.

DIRECTOR: Right. We're trying to decorate, it's an American yurt but it does have the right shape to it. We've been told by several students from Kyrgyzstan and all that we would be considered a very poor family given the size of our yurt [laughs, then speaks as if a tour guide]. "This is a very small yurt, it would be an extremely poor family." But we are trying at least to decorate it in the style of central Asia.

The two went on to describe how they display the yurt at events throughout the year, calling it "wonderful outreach." "People just come through [saying], 'what is this?' you know, 'what is this tent thing?' And so we get flyers on what a yurt is and, as you said, [the] rugs and so forth are all authentic that we have inside, they are all from central Asia."

The evolution of the academic organization of Middle East studies offers a clear example of the cumulative character of academic activity. Middle East studies was the core focus of our empirical inquiry, not least because the region's prominent place in contemporary geopolitics had placed it front and center in debates about area studies programs throughout the mid-2000s. Public interest in the Middle East region was on the rise, and national news was filled with reports on the wars in Iraq and Afghanistan. We had anticipated that the national schema might be especially prominent in the academic organization of Middle East studies. We found that these programs betrayed all three schemata simultaneously.

Civilizational approaches to the study of the Middle East have prominently endured in the form of Near Eastern studies programs; specialist faculty in humanities and history departments; and in occasionally spectacular collections of books, manuscripts, and other historical artifacts. Middle East studies center directors, who were often humanists or historians themselves, invoked these assets in interviews as evidence of their universities' academic strengths. They repeatedly talked about their centers' role in educating the public in ways that echoed the civilizational schema's emphasis on the creation of enlightened citizens. "I think that it's a really important time for people to be educated about [the region] and not just what they hear on the news and not just the bad things that everyone has been hearing the last couple of years," said one Middle East center staff member. "Our primary goal is to educate people about something we see as being important. Also for the future of our country and the world, I think it's important. It should have happened a long time ago," she said, going on to suggest that tragic events in recent history might have played out differently if Americans had been better informed about the region.

Inheriting the civilizational schema's notion that studying others civilizes oneself, directors often invoked their role as enlightening educators. A Middle East center director elsewhere said:

> Frankly, it would be useful to have more of a deeper understanding preached to the American public. That this is not a matter of "we need to know how to kill them better" and therefore we need to know "Raise your hands" in Arabic and Farsi and Turkish, and "Don't move or we'll machine gun you." We don't need that kind of knowledge. We need deep knowledge. . . . We are fated to have encounters with these regions, South Asia and the Middle East in particular. And by fated, I mean harsh, confrontational, thousands-of-people-slaughtered-annually-encounters, in the Middle East and South Asia because we are going to be at war in Afghanistan and Central Asia and parts of the Middle East, on and off, for the most of our lifetimes. If we can help to avert the worst parts of that, ameliorate it, and stop it ideally through deep knowledge, we'll be serving humanity, and this country. End of speech.

When invoking this civilizing obligation, center administrators frequently referenced their duties to specific constituencies. A director of a Middle East center elsewhere explained that he thought of his center as serving three "circles":

> The first circle is service to the university community . . . the second circle is the local community . . . and then the third circle is that national circle, we do what we can to provide the larger American

community, whether official or unofficial, with information about the Middle East and ways of thinking about the Middle East.

Another believed that part of his charge "with our Title VI money is to educate people and to produce educated, intelligent citizens and educated, intelligent citizens need to know how to criticize, so if we want to criticize we should be able to do that, and it worries me that there is a kind of question mark over our right to do that." He later elaborated that "yes this is something that is running with federal funds, but we consider it a very important part of our national responsibility to teach people how to be critical."

Middle East studies centers funded by Title VI have a categorical obligation to serve the "national interest" however it may be officially defined by the US federal government. Personnel in Middle East centers clearly understood their obligations to make tangible contributions to government service. They made frequent reference to the production and use of knowledge for US policy through the formal training of students. "There is a huge demand for Arabic in this country driven by Homeland Security, driven by the war in Iraq, driven by many things, driven by the intelligence of kids who want to learn the language because they know it is going to be needed," said one director. Others talked about the strategic value of foreign languages, particularly in relation to the federal government's incentive for funding centers. ". . . When it comes to . . . Title VI they want us to think about, 'we are giving you this money, what payback do we get for this money?'" said one center director in a joint interview. His associate replied, "You get a pool of strategic language speakers."

An associate director of a Middle East center at an elite private university talked about brokering jobs in government service:

> There definitely is that sense coming from outside the university that if the government is funding programs in Middle Eastern Studies then those programs should be producing people who are going to be actively working for the interest of the United States, however that's defined. I'll give you a very micro instance of the way that's affected some of the things I do because as director of the master's program I do put together these career workshops, and I do make more of a concerted effort now to get government agencies in to pitch careers to our students. So we had the FBI come last month, we have someone from the State Department come. . . . I am in touch with someone now to try and get someone from the CIA to come, because . . . it's irrelevant whatever my personal opinions are of those kinds of careers, the fact is if we have students who are interested in those kinds of careers, I want to enable them.

Beyond the contributions of their own units, center personnel occasionally suggested that the universities employing them could bend in the direction of national service. The director of the Middle East center—the person to whom the above speaker reported—suggested changes in departmental hiring priorities in the wake of recent Middle East conflicts: "Everybody . . . is aware of the fact that here is a university that has an international reputation at a time when the Middle East has become a main focus for American foreign policy . . . not having anyone in the Government department teaching Middle East government or Islamic politics . . . you can only run so many searches and you have priorities, and for a while the Middle East wasn't a high priority to [the] Government [department]; now it is."

The service relationship between universities and government implicit in Title VI funding did not always sit well with center personnel. This was evident in terse remarks about general aptitude in government intelligence, such as this one, from a Middle East center director at a large public flagship university:

> One of the problems [in the intelligence community] is that they have no depth to what they know about the region. It's very model driven, formula driven, assuming that everyone everywhere behaves in a certain way and just thinking you can export one model from one country to another and not knowing the languages, not knowing the history, not knowing the culture, any of these things which are part of the analysis. Certainly they need other tools as well. But a lot of that they can get on the job training once they get out there. But you know, they are not going to learn anything about broader trends in nationalism or state formation or authoritarian regimes. They are not going to learn any of that on the job in the State Department or the CIA. They are going to learn all of that here. And the specifics of how to chase down a terrorist in a network, that they will learn there.

Or there is this comment, from an associate director at an elite private university, about the shortsightedness of government funders:

> You know, in fifteen years, when something blows out of the water in Kazakhstan, somebody is going to be screaming, "why don't we have anybody who speaks Kazakh?!" And . . . we're going to have to say, "well because you took all the funding from the Kazakh program . . ."

Even while their centers' livelihoods were predicated on federal funds, personnel hardly presumed official national interests and priorities were in line with their own.

Nor did they presume that all of the academic activity pertinent to regional inquiry happened through area studies centers. The universities in which our respondents lived and worked were spectacularly ornate organizations. They had become infamous for their sprawling variety of programs, byzantine cross-subsidies, contradictory missions, and anarchic governance.[50] Organizational marvels they certainly are, but neither coral reefs nor research universities can appropriately be called rational. So it did not surprise us that center directors often used terms like "very unique," "curious," or "complex" to describe the character of their administrative relations with other units—or that they were only loosely connected, if at all, with other university initiatives in their target regions. As one director of Middle East studies put it:

> If the law school were going to establish a branch [overseas] I doubt they would ask us, and certainly the medical school, which is establishing medical outposts all over the place, is not interested in us at all. . . . It just doesn't occur to them, and I think it may be the way the world works globally. I mean you get on a plane and you go to Dubai . . . when you get there you stay in the Sheraton or something . . . they don't observe that there is any need to attend to local worries . . . the cultural intermediary role that we might have played once I don't think exists very much.

Working in universities with myriad and ever changing programs, center personnel could not take for granted that they would get academic planners' first calls. Phenomena that might once have been imagined as belonging to regionally specific programs could be framed in new ways. A senior international officer at a large flagship public university told us that he aimed to "de-center" traditional topics associated with Middle East studies: "De-centering in the sense that, for example, studying Islam, for the relatively ignorant, would seem to fit in very well with Middle Eastern studies, but as we all know, that's not true." He stressed that the study of Islam often was undertaken outside the confines of the Middle East studies center, and reflected on the university's approach "not to exclusively focus on the Middle East, not to exclusively focus on radical Islam, but to see the whole thing in kind of global comparative perspective."

⁂

In the end what may be most remarkable about regional inquiry in the US academy is the hybridity of its multiple legacies. The study of regions has taken many forms and definitions, changing over time

as universities negotiate their relationships with the federal government and other patrons and—as we will see in subsequent chapters—
compete ever more fiercely with one another for resources and prestige in the present day. Organizational capacity and ways of thinking
built under the civilizational and national schemata powerfully endure in our now officially "global" age. The Cold War was especially
definitive for the academic present, and because of this we devote a
few more pages looking back on some critical decades in the evolution of regional knowledge.

CHAPTER 2

What Is Area Studies?

Nor are the facts of culture history without bearing on the judgement of our own future. To that planless hodgepodge, that thing of shreds and patches called civilization, its historian can no longer yield superstitious reverence. He will realize better than others the obstacles to infusing design into the amorphous product; but in thought at least he will not grovel before it in fatalistic acquiescence but dream of a rational scheme to supplant the chaotic jumble.
—ROBERT LOWIE, 1920

To borrow from anthropologist Robert Lowie,[1] in the civilizational academy the rest of the world is a "planless hodgepodge" of "shreds and patches" of others, assembled on the place of a campus for scholarly consideration. Yet as early as Lowie's time, the seeds of a different way of making sense of the world had already been planted, "a rational scheme to supplant the chaotic jumble." What became the dominant means of defining knowledge of others by the middle of the twentieth century was modernization theory, whose guiding ambitions of international development and domestic security defined the production of knowledge about the rest of the world as a substantially coherent project of national service. In a powerful commingling of scholarly ambition, philanthropic coordination, and government mandate, advocates of modernization theory created a new academic infrastructure that would endure for generations.

The first third of the twentieth century had seen the coalescence of the core machinery of social knowledge production in US universities: the delineation and consolidation of disciplines.[2] The emergence of economics, political science, and sociology as distinct fields came with a strong focus on US society. The defining topics of these social sciences were domestic problems: industrialization, immigration, urban change and "social hygiene," and the development of the institutions of modern capitalism.[3] In the decades before World War II, academic study of the rest of the world, as well as of "others" within such as Native Americans, was largely relegated to adherents of the older civilizational schema as expressed in anthropology and Oriental studies, both of which took on disciplinary definition but were rarely in dialogue with the social sciences. During and after World War II, however, many economists, political scientists, and sociologists lent fresh attention to the world beyond the United States, endeavoring to rationalize civilizational approaches to the study of the culture, languages, and history of other places. During the Cold War the organizational architecture devised for housing much of this work was "area studies" in the form of interdisciplinary centers—not departments, as we will discuss in Chapter 3—specifically purposed with bringing social science expertise to bear on the development of regions beyond US national borders.

Because the organizational architecture of area studies was so fateful for how universities would encourage social knowledge production from that time forward, we offer a schematic view of the area studies project as it coalesced in the middle of the twentieth century. Our effort draws on a generous secondary literature, as well as on Seteney Shami's career of experience in scaffolding regional inquiry through serial appointments at the Social Science Research Council. Addressing this chapter's title question, we offer three answers. First, area studies was a component of the massive scientific/intellectual movement that was modernization theory. This movement comprised myriad coordinated contributions from ambitious academics, a philanthropic sector encouraging applied social science, the US Congress, multiple federal agencies, and several presidential administrations. Area studies as we came to examine them cannot be properly understood independently of this movement. Second, from their Cold War inception, area studies have been a controversial academic project, existing at twin interstices: between general and particularistic knowledge and between universities and the state. This complicated position is central to how many regional specialists perceive their status in the US academic world. Third, as funded by the US federal government, area studies created the organizational model of the interdisciplinary center—an enduring legacy of the modernization project and a now indispensable tool for university planners.

A Scientific/Intellectual Movement

Sociologists Scott Frickel and Neil Gross define scientific/intellectual movements (SIMs) as "collective efforts to pursue research programs or projects for thought in the face of resistance from others in the scientific or intellectual community." They continue:

At their core, SIMs have a more or less coherent program for scientific or intellectual change or advance. However conceptualized and implemented, these programs involve the transformation of thoughts or research findings into ideas and knowledge that are circulated widely within the intellectual community, subjected to scrutiny and contestation, embraced by some and rejected by others, and that may emerge from the process deemed credible or true.[4]

Frickel and Gross developed the SIM concept to integrate insights from the study of social movements with the sociology of ideas. While our synoptic view here can hardly do scholarly justice to modernization theory as a social/intellectual movement, we believe that the SIM concept is a useful frame for understanding the creation of area studies programs as we came to examine them. The SIM concept also broadly comports with the growing historical literature on the Cold War academy upon which we rely for our admittedly brief account here.[5]

Through their consultative engagements with the US military during the first and second world wars, US social scientists learned to appreciate just how substantial government patronage for academic endeavors might be. Psychologists showed special alacrity in finding ways to be of use to the military. They benefitted handsomely through their development of many tests of individual fitness for wartime service, tools for human-resource management during wartime, and for "readjustment" to civilian life at war's end.[6] While economists, sociologists, and political scientists also benefitted from contracts for services related to war efforts, it was not until the conclusion of World War II and the early decades of the Cold War that federal patronage would definitively influence the evolution of these disciplines.[7]

The broad strokes of the organizational blueprint for social science research on world regions were drawn by the Social Science Research Council (SSRC), a New York–based philanthropy founded in 1923 with the express purpose of bringing scholarly expertise to bear on the crafting of enlightened public policy. From its inception the SSRC did its work through a "committee" structure in which groups of experts were charged with specifying substantive domains for research inquiry and securing funding for them from government and private agencies. The inaugural SSRC committees were charged with investigating "Interracial Relations, Scientific Aspects of Human Migration, and the Eighteenth Amendment [banning the sale of alcohol]."[8] In the wake of World War II, the SSRC ambitiously expanded its mandate to include the encouragement of US social scientific inquiry that might inform social policy worldwide. This moment is where any account of area studies as a scientific/intellectual movement of social scientists properly begins.[9]

In 1947 the SSRC published geographer Robert B. Hall's influential *Area Studies: With Special Reference to Their Implications for Research in the Social Sciences*, sponsored by the SSRC's "Exploratory Committee on World Areas Research." It proposed the need for broad educational changes to counter scholarly ignorance concerning world regions. The SSRC had already established the "Committee on Latin American Studies" in 1942, followed in 1949 by the "Committee on Slavic and East European Studies" and the "Committee on Southern Asia." The year 1959 saw committees on "Contemporary China," the "Near and Middle East," and "African Studies." But the effort that cast the longest shadow over the future of area studies was the "Committee on Comparative Politics" (CCP), co-founded in 1954 by political scientists Pendleton Herring from Harvard and Gabriel Almond, then of Princeton and founder of Princeton's Center for International Studies.

In the words of Cold War historian Nils Gilman, the CCP "helped to fashion the emerging scholarly consensus on modernization theory":

> These scholars would take an existing field of scholarship, the comparative study of political institutions in traditional great powers, and transform it into a field dedicated to understanding how the politics of the postcolonial world differed from that of the industrialized world. To do this, they would develop a new theoretical foundation for comparative politics, drawing on the theorizing being done at the [Department of Social Relations at Harvard] about the nature of modernity and the process through which nations achieved modernity[.][10]

The CCP and the other SSRC area committees were part of a larger effort to connect the ambitions of a few elite social scientists with the massive capacity and global reach of the US federal government. Harvard University, unquestionably the center of the North American academic universe in mid-century, was a major site for this endeavor. It was there that a network of social scientists centered on sociologist Talcott Parsons pursued a decades-long project of building a coherent theoretical conception of modernity—and an empirical program for investigating its progress. Their work included the creation of an interdisciplinary Department of Social Relations and a compelling way of thinking about the evolution of societies in the twentieth century that came to be called modernization theory.

In its most general outline, modernization theory posited that nation-states outside of the industrialized West might be made to progress more rapidly in their economic and political development with thoughtful inputs of resources and expertise from countries already at later stages of the process. Academic social science was presumed to be essential to this endeavor, because inducing development properly required rigorous theorizing about modernization as a general phenomenon, as well as systematic empirical inquiry into the evolution of particular societies. Modernization scholars inherited the optimism and scientism of the Progressive reformers who had been instrumental in creating the US social sciences at the turn of the twentieth century, and the more enduring Enlightenment faith in rational inquiry to improve the human condition. But they made two pivotal additions to these traditions. First, they conceptualized modernity as the result of a *process* that could be empirically observed and assessed comparatively with systematic evidence. Second, they endeavored to link their scientific/intellectual movement directly to the geopolitical ambitions of the US federal government. In a remarkable coalescence of academic and philanthropic ambitions and geopolitical uncertainty, modernization theory emerged as a simultaneously intellectual and national-security project.

Much of the impetus for federal government support of the modernization movement can be traced to US embarrassment over the lack of adequate intelligence about the Soviet Union as the Cold War began. In 1948 the Central Intelligence Agency housed thirty-eight Soviet analysts, two-thirds of whom spoke no Russian, and only one of whom held a doctoral degree.[11] As geopolitical tensions with the USSR intensified, a coalition of government leaders, private foundations, and national organizations including the American Council of Learned Societies (ACLS) began to brainstorm ways to incentivize knowledge production on world regions to strengthen US expertise on foreign places and peoples. At the same time the Soviet Union was investing in building a starkly different conception of social progress and offering it to newly postcolonial states.[12]

By the 1960s, modernization theory was the guiding intellectual framework for US foreign policy in what was often called the "third" or "developing" world. Adherents of many different disciplines took up modernization theory, each within their domain of expertise.[13] The intellectual historian Michael Latham summarizes it this way:

> Modernization was not simply a rhetorical strategy invoked to legitimate government actions. The high degree of continuity between private, policymaking materials and public interpretation

reveals that it was also a conceptual framework. Modernization shaped specific practices and articulated widely shared beliefs about the nature of the United States, its ethical duty, and its ability to direct global change. Embedded in social scientific discourse, foreign policy institutions, and forms of cultural representation, it promised to accelerate the "progress" of a world requiring America's resources and enlightened tutelage.[14]

Government support for social scientific inquiry on specific world regions during the Cold War was a direct result and enduring legacy of this social/intellectual movement.

Initially authorized through the National Defense Education Act of 1958, Title VI provided the first federal funding for centers purposed with fostering regional expertise.[15] The funds came on the heels of an effort coordinated by the SSRC and major US foundations, including Carnegie, Ford, and Rockefeller, to encourage the training of specialists in world regions deemed important to national security interests. Within a few years Title VI received ongoing funding as part of the Higher Education Act of 1965. Its mandate remained the same: to create experts in world regions, world affairs, and international studies. In this, knowledge of languages and culture was seen as central. Area studies programs as they are now known owe their existence to Title VI.[16]

Title VI created National Resource Centers (NRCs) on university campuses across the country. NRCs were charged with providing academic instruction and language training on world regions, particularly in the Soviet bloc but also Latin and South America, Africa, South Asia, and the Middle East.[17] The creation of NRCs firmly established regional inquiry as a broad approach to teaching and studying places beyond US borders, and provided ongoing organizational support for social scientists' systematic attention to the non-Western world. For many of their early champions, regional inquiry supported by NRCs had the potential to integrate the study of "traditional" and "modern" societies. Echoing earlier civilizational notions of unilinear cultural evolution, modernization theory positioned the non-Western world as being on the same trajectory toward modernity as the West—with at least somewhat shared futures of democratization, industrialization, secularization, and consumerism. In this vision the United States was seen as a more reliable guide than the older democracies of Western Europe. As the back jacket of sociologist Seymour Martin Lipset's germinal 1963 book, *The First New Nation*, put it: "The U.S. was the first major colony to revolt successfully against colonial rule. In this sense, it was the first 'new nation'."[18]

The world according to NRCs was divided into clearly specified nations and regions. The very existence of the centers encouraged a view of the expertise under their purview as context-specific—as being "about" Eastern Europe, East Asia, Africa, and Latin America, for example. In this the NRCs embodied a presumption of regional coherence from the civilizational schema. As shaped by comparative-politics social scientists, however, the unit of analysis was not the civilization and its territory, but the nation-state and its sovereign capacity. Further, research on particular nation-states would often be elided into "regional" analyses: India would often be the simulacrum of South Asia; Russian studies were equated with research on the USSR; Egypt, Turkey, or Iran (depending on a scholar's own reference group) might stand in for the Middle East. Cores and peripheries were created and debated within each "area," while definitions of "area" and "region" tended to presume an ontology of the nation-state.

Though it is not a focus of our own inquiry, we would be remiss not to note an important variation across area studies fields. This variation has partly to do with the strategic importance of any given region for US national interests during the Cold War. The studies of the Soviet Union and Latin America both mattered for US foreign policy, but in very different ways. The academic priors of Cold War area studies are also fateful for their subsequent evolution. Civilizational inquiry is a powerful legacy for Middle East and (via Sanskrit) South Asian studies, much less so for programs on Latin America and Africa. By dint of its implication in European colonialism, anthropological approaches to scholarship are relatively more common in African studies programs. Each area studies field battles its own ghosts of the past as well as the geopolitical demands of its present in ways that create different thematic priorities, disciplinary configurations, and methodological predilections.

A Controversial Academic Project

Situated both between academic traditions and between the university and the state, area studies and their denizen experts have long faced intellectual, political, and organizational uncertainty.[19] Even while the first generation of social scientists to champion regional inquiry during the Cold War did so from the most prestigious heights of their disciplines, it did not take long for latter-day detractors to criticize regionally focused inquiry for being overly descriptive, atheoretical, and "soft."[20] As Mark Tessler and his colleagues put it, at the heart of an ongoing debate between regional specialists and disciplinary generalists has been "social science epistemology, about what constitutes, or should constitute, the paradigm by which scholars construct knowledge about politics, economics, and international relations in major world regions."[21] Sociologist John Lie says it more bluntly: "[S]ocial scientists by and large belittle area studies as repositories of particularistic knowledge," while area studies scholars often return the favor, viewing "sociologists or economists with generalizing ethos . . . as yahoos for whom the concern with abstraction loosens their grip on concrete reality." [22] We take up the tension between disciplinary versus regionally focused scholarship in detail in Chapter 5.

More broadly, intellectual historians agree that critiques of modernization arose almost as quickly as the movement itself. Proponents of modernization would often be called out for their ethnocentrism or complicity with US military agendas—and worse—by academic critics.[23] And as government-funded enterprises, area studies were explicitly political from the start. Latin American experts caught an early wave of it following Project Camelot, a 1960s US military-funded research project to study counterinsurgency tactics and revolutionary movements.[24] South Asianists would receive similar treatment during the US war in Vietnam. More recently, Middle East studies has faced substantial public criticism, particularly from many on the political right who have accused Middle East studies scholars for being unpatriotic or for failing to predict the emergence of radical Islamic terrorism.[25]

Recent scholarship has explored in detail how such controversy has played out in the case of Middle East studies.[26] The field's current fate has been indelibly defined by 9/11, the wars in Iraq and Afghanistan, and the emergence of al Qaeda and ISIS as global terror threats. Government funding priorities for scholarship on the Middle East shifted, with knowledge and instruction incentivized more explicitly for purposes of US national security. Overlapping but less regionally specific fields of study would subsequently emerge: security studies, research centers for terrorism and deradicalization, and a reoriented Islamic studies field.

As we detail in the methodological appendix, the broader project of which this book is a part focused on four world regions: Russia/Eurasia, South Asia, the Middle East, and Central Asia. Middle East studies was our central focus, in part because it remains one of the most contested and politically charged fields today. As an academic domain, Middle East studies is roiled with ongoing tension and critique from both within and without. Internally, Middle East studies scholars are highly critical of the field's origins in civilizational approaches and the continuing legacies of orientalism and colonialism in university departments and museum collections. As we described in Chapter 1, the organizational structures housing civilizational inquiry were not supplanted. Instead capacity for Cold War area studies was built alongside them.

From the vantage point of regional inquiry, it is revealing to compare the national schema at the end of the Cold War with the period following 9/11. In the first, Soviet studies bore the brunt of the shock for not having "predicted" the fall of the Berlin Wall, while Middle East studies was criticized for not having "predicted" 9/11. Soviet studies saw a period of disarray when "the very existence of a discernible community of scholars focusing on the societies, cultures, and political and economic systems of the various states and territories that were under the control of the Soviet regime is in question"[27]—or, even more starkly, that "Sovietology . . . is in the soup."[28] That moment eventually passed. By the end of the decade, the same community had reorganized, first as "post-Soviet studies" and sometime later and more awkwardly under a variety of descriptive rubrics with different combinations of Eastern Europe, Eurasia, Russia, and Central Asia. In 2010, the main area studies association for the region changed its name from The American Association for the Advancement of Slavic Studies (AAASS) to its current Association for Slavic, East European, and Eurasian Studies (ASEEES).

Still, it was only after about 2010 that federal funding for the "post-Soviet" space began to dry up, although after 9/11 there was a widespread perception that funds were being shifted from Russia/Eurasia toward the Middle East. This perception was not based entirely in reality although important shifts did take place in the structures of funding. Already in the 1990s, Title VIII, an important program funding research and training for the region, administered by the State Department, dropped the Baltic States from the definition of their region, since these had "become" part of Europe and the Eastern European countries also began to be less of a priority for federal funds. A steady shift in focus and invitational priorities for funding began to take place toward Central Asia and Russia.

Because they exist at the interstices of two substantial tensions—between the disciplinary and the regional, and between universities and the state—those who make their careers in area studies continually feel the need to defend their status in the academic world. The fieldwork that informs the other chapters of this book took place during years of area studies' waning as the dominant paradigm for organizing knowledge about the world within US universities. In addition, our interviews were conducted at a time when the 9/11 attacks and their potential implications for government funding of regional inquiry were fresh in the minds of many with whom we spoke. Discussion of national needs for research relevant to security and for expertise on specific world regions was being reiterated in many quarters. Debate, often polemical and bitter, over how federal funding should be used for promoting such knowledge occupied the attention of many regional specialists. Seen in this light, the strong emotional valences of many interview utterances—cynicism, gallows humor, resignation, anger— are more understandable.

An Enduring Organizational Form

Despite these constitutional tensions, every major US research university today bears traces of the area studies project: through NRCs, other research centers defined by the study of world regions, or faculty lines tied to world-regional specialization. Most important, the area studies project brought an organizational model—the center—which would have diffuse and enduring consequences for academic planning into the present. In Chapter 3 we take up the generic organizational characteristics of centers, or, as we call them, "not-departments." Here we provide an overview of what centers funded by Title VI do.

NRCs serve several functions that typically do not fall within disciplinary departments. We detail four of those functions here: language training, public outreach, support for research abroad, and general encouragement of regional inquiry.

Language training. A central mandate of Title VI is to ensure national capacity in foreign languages. NRCs act as the implementing body for this mandate.[29] They coordinate much of the language training offered on university campuses, often employing adjunct faculty to ensure that needs for less commonly taught languages (LCTLs) are met. In many cases, NRCs coordinate instruction of more heavily enrolled language courses as well. They conduct the competitions for federally funded Foreign Language and Area Studies (FLAS) grants, which fund graduate students to study languages at institutions overseas in the summer months or fund full-academic year fellowships for graduate study that includes foreign language training at the home campus.

Public outreach. Title VI funding for NRCs comes with an explicit mandate for "outreach." NRCs are required to provide information and/or consultation to local, state, and national partners, particularly to other postsecondary schools in their region that do not have

NRC funding, as well as to the business community, the general public, and elementary and secondary schools.[30] Although outreach itself is defined broadly and includes public events and community workshops, official invitational priorities in Title VI grant competitions have had the effect of focusing outreach on particular kinds of activity. For example, some grant competitions have singled out teacher training, partnerships with schools of education, and partnerships with K–12 schools as priorities.[31] Extending the knowledge gained through NRC work downward into K–12 schools is understood to be a key part of the overall mission of NRCs to seed expertise on world regions. NRCs routinely draw on faculty and graduate student experts to run summer teacher training programs, provide classroom speakers, develop curriculum guides and professional-development workshops, and run teacher study abroad trips to target regions. The cumulative result is that NRCs have been "incubators of many texts, reference grammars and dictionaries, curricular materials, and websites for extending area, global and language knowledge into the K–12 institutions, colleges, and universities across the land."[32]

Scholarly mobility. NRCs systematically assist students and faculty with scholarly mobility to and from their target regions.[33] Centers host visiting scholars and experts for campus stays, offering support that might include assistance with visas and housing, the provision of stipends, arrangement of teaching opportunities, and office space. NRCs also build and maintain formal partnerships with organizations in their target regions, helping facilitate study abroad and student exchange programs, internships, research collaborations, and access to archives. NRCs fund student and faculty mobility through FLAS and other awards for doctoral and undergraduate research, travel, and conferences.

Space. NRCs are not only virtual collections of coursework and clearinghouses of information about how to spend time overseas. They are also physical places where students and faculty with interest in the target regions can gather for academic, cultural, and social events. Unscheduled use is consequential as well; students and faculty alike spoke of the importance of lounges, couches, and reception areas as sites of interaction contributing to their intellectual growth.[34]

There is no uniform approach to the physical location of NRCs and other area studies centers. Some are grouped together in a central location underneath a larger organizational umbrella, such as an international institute or a school of international studies, while others are placed in buildings at some remove from one another. An enduring legacy of the civilizational schema, these spaces often are decorated with objects connoting their regions: Middle Eastern mosaics, Mexican tiles, African carvings, Asian tapestries. Some are prominently housed in central campus locations, while others have nondescript addresses in basements or distant buildings that are unlikely to be encountered by anyone not pursuing them as specific destinations. NRC staff talked openly about how their physical facilities signaled their relative status.[35]

It is hard to overestimate the impact of area studies on the organization of regional knowledge in the US academy. "The most notable academic innovation after 1945 was the creation of area studies as a new institutional category to group intellectual work," asserts Immanuel Wallerstein, explaining that as regional scholars came together to create curriculum, advise doctoral students, attend conferences, and publish in new journals, they created capacity for scaffolding knowledge that transcended longstanding divides. "Whatever the intellectual value of this cross-fertilization," he continues, "the organizational consequences for the social sciences were immense."[36] We agree. Even while the scientific/intellectual movement that gave rise to area studies has faded, the organizational form it brought into being endures.[37] In a contemporary academic world in which interdisciplinarity is treated by academic patrons and planners as a "philosopher's stone, capable of turning vulgar metals into gold," this is a significant legacy.[38]

CHAPTER 3

Departments and Not-Departments

A research university is a thousand wishes, a pile of ambitions. Faculty members pursue theirs by securing time, space, money, colleagues, and students. Generally speaking, faculty always want more: more research funding, more colleagues in their own field, more office and lab space, more generous support packages for the recruitment of more capable doctoral students, more exemptions from teaching. Academic management means finding ways to link ambitious faculty with available resources, all the while minding that patrons and students get reasonable return on their own investments of gifts, grants, and tuition.[1]

Generations of sociologists have considered how this management happens in the physical, natural, and medical sciences, but only recently have they lent sustained attention to parallel activity in the social sciences and humanities.[2] This is important because the production functions of the social sciences and humanities are rather peculiar. First, production costs in these fields are vastly lower than elsewhere in academia. Unlike in many of the sciences, huge investments in fancy equipment or battalions of postdocs are not required to make top-drawer sociology or art history.[3] Second, whereas the physical, natural, and medical sciences have deep-pocketed clients in government and industry, social scientists and humanists face much weaker demand for their expertise beyond the academy. They do not make medicines or machines. Consequently, squarely scholarly measures of accomplishment—publication in top journals primarily, but also doctoral student job placements and undergraduate enrollments—are the nearly exclusive priorities for faculty and administrators in the social sciences and humanities. Third, these programs inherit pride of place at the symbolic heart of US universities, comprising most of what is typically regarded as a liberal arts education. Premier medicine and engineering programs may pay a lot of the bills, but few universities reach the top ranks without excellence in the humanities and social sciences.

In 2001, University of Chicago sociologist Andrew Abbott made a compelling argument about knowledge production at this academic core. He explained how the "dual institutionalization" of academic disciplines and university departments near the beginning of the twentieth century created a remarkably durable system for dividing intellectual labor, rationalizing academic labor markets, and organizing undergraduate instruction simultaneously.[4] Insightful as it is, Abbott's analysis provides only minimal account of the academic activity that happens outside of, and in between, departments and disciplines. We are referring here not only or even primarily to the much-discussed intellectual projects of interdisciplinarity, but also to the academic units universities build adjacent to departments. To honor our inheritance of Abbott's work and forward its critical extension, we call these units *not-departments*. Fully recognizing these ubiquitous features of university life provides a much richer vision of scholarly production and politics at the heart of US universities.

In what follows we first offer a synopsis of Abbott's analysis of departments and disciplines. We concur with Abbott's essential insights but also note the limitations of a theory of academic knowledge production premised exclusively on departments as legitimate university units. Next we synthetically describe not-departments— the extraordinarily flexible, highly legitimate organizational devices faculty and administrators alike have long used to pursue their ambitions. The area studies centers funded by Title VI are paradigmatic instances of not-departments: interdisciplinary; topic focused; and amenable to expansion, contraction, and redefinition with changing circumstances.

Next we listen to center leaders explain the utilities and fragilities of their not-department enterprises. This testimony gives telling insight into the complex production function of the academic core. As one might expect, not-departments provide myriad practical resources for the accomplishment of disciplinary scholarship. Less obviously, they enable universities to manage the academic prestige system's obdurate contradiction between disciplinary and client service. This management system has important consequences for academics' professional status. We conclude by suggesting how the department/not-department binary is linked with academic identity.

Departments and Disciplines

The division of scholarly labor into academic disciplines is neither an inevitable nor longstanding phenomenon. As Abbott and others before us have explained in detail, the humanistic and social science disciplines as they are known today are products of the remarkable ferment of US higher education around the beginning of the twentieth century. During this period American academics and their college-founding patrons in government and industry were eager to create institutions matching Germany's in research prestige. The German ideal of universities as enlightening educators and knowledge producers was embraced in a young nation optimistic about its capacity to invent, or discover, a prosperous future. But as an organizational technology the German university was a tough sell in the United States. It was unabashedly intellectual, inheriting an enduring cultural reverence for scholarship that would never fully take hold in a nation founded by religious iconoclasts and businesspeople. Americans valued colleges to the extent that they were useful for training ministers and teachers, improving crop yields and settling frontiers. Further, German universities were rigidly hierarchical, giving a relatively small number of senior faculty great discretion over junior scholars, research programs, and curriculum. Although it was briefly attempted by a few early US universities, faculty oligarchy on the German model would prove untenable in America, where academic governance had been broadly distributed among faculty, affluent philanthropists, and (at public institutions) state legislatures from the very beginning.[5]

Even while they envied the intellectual heights achieved by German universities, Americans also maintained admiration for the English model of residential colleges focused on undergraduates. The practice of physically sequestering young college men, often in bucolic locations, fit well with the utopian religious traditions so many American intellectuals inherited. Early American colleges were often imagined as lights of idealized civilization in the New World and on the Western frontier. The gradual hybridization of the German research and English undergraduate residential models into a specifically American academic form is one of the central themes of US higher education history.[6]

As Abbott explains in detail, the Americans' focus on undergraduates and their desire to make academics useful encouraged the development of a nationally peculiar invention: the college major. In America, becoming educated meant becoming educated about something that might be of practical value to students and their industries, families, and communities. So alongside and ultimately in place of the traditional Greek and Latin, specific courses of study were developed in fields heretofore unheard of in Europe: animal husbandry, business, and home economics, for example. Academic leaders developed utilitarian programs of study in order to sate public expectations for utility, but they also recognized other benefits to a management structure organized around majors and disciplines. Domain concentrations better enabled preparation for advanced study in particular fields. Making successful completion of a particular program of study a prerequisite for advanced training enabled senior scholars to do more with their acolytes. It is not coincidental that the development of the college major was exactly contemporaneous with the tiering of US higher education into undergraduate and graduate/professional strata.[7]

The college major had deep consequences for national academic organization. First, it rationalized the intramural management of faculty labor. Undergraduate enrollments in particular courses and subjects became fundamental components of university accounting and human-capital allocation. Administrators distributed faculty appointments in the academic units delivering instruction in particular programs of study. Second, it rationalized national labor markets for faculty, as departments recruited new hires with specifically disciplinary training.[8] Third, the college major encouraged the rationalization of knowledge production itself into specifically disciplinary domains. Because young scholars seeking faculty appointments entered labor markets organized by discipline, they developed expertise and produced research specifically defined along disciplinary lines. So, for example, the intellectual complexity of the domain once called political economy became much more crisply delineated by the terminological and methodological differences among economics, history, political science, and sociology. Social science itself became disciplinary.[9]

Another consequence of the major system was intramural competition among academic programs for majors. Because deans and provosts distribute faculty appointments at least partly on the basis of undergraduate enrollments, few departments are exempt from minding their undergraduate numbers. Even while the disciplinary status systems reward faculty on the basis of their research productivity, local resource allocation systems mean that department leaders also covet high enrollments and teaching evaluations.

As Abbott explained, all of these processes are interdependent and mutually reinforcing. The college major encourages a particular managerial structure within universities, which provides incentives for disciplinary specification and specialization, which abets disciplinary boundaries in labor markets and departmental competitions, which further induce homophily within disciplines. So deep are these interdependencies and so embedded in the institutional structure of US higher education that Abbott called the overall system "virtually unbreakable."[10]

Since the 1990s the steadily rising popularity of national and global academic ranking systems has only abetted these dynamics. Academic leaders and patrons increasingly turn to the numerical ratings of third parties to assess the relative performance of particular academic programs. Almost invariably, the subunits subjected to rankings are professional schools and academic departments in the arts-and-sciences core. It is not the academic fields of business or humanities or social science that are the units of analysis for raters, but *schools* of business and *departments* of economics or sociology. This fact trains administrative attention to disciplinary departments as primary units for investment in pursuit of prestige.[11]

Abbott's analysis is elegant, parsimonious, and compelling. To our knowledge it has no serious detractors in the sociology of knowledge and has deeply shaped subsequent scholarship far beyond our own.[12] Yet it is empirically incomplete. It is about departments, to the exclusion of the many other academic units that populate the organizational diagrams of research universities. These units go by many names. *Institute* is one enduring moniker, used for example by the esteemed Oriental Institute at Abbott's University of Chicago, founded in 1919 for the study of the ancient Middle East. There is *center*, brought into common academic parlance by the Title VI–funded programs that are the vehicle for our inquiry here. *Project, forum, network,* and *lab* are more recently fashionable terms, whose numbers reflect the ubiquity of the units they describe throughout the firmament of US higher education. The name we use here recognizes something all of these units have in common. None of them are departments.

A useful way to appreciate the ontology of not-departments is to consider what they tend not to have: tenure lines, doctoral programs, and academic self-governance. Of these three the signal absence is tenured appointments.

Guaranteed life employment, awarded through departments and schools on the basis of scholarly productivity, was the settlement Americans made with the German academic model. US universities were not to be oligarchies of faculty. Instead they became caste systems, with tenured professors as the Brahmins. There can be little question that tenured faculty are any university's most privileged citizens. They can spend time and other resources at their disposal largely as they wish. They can recruit and train doctoral students more or less as they see fit. Perhaps most importantly, they play a substantial role in their own generational replacement: at their home institutions, by selecting junior faculty and assessing them for promotion; and in their disciplines more broadly by evaluating tenure cases and grooming their own protégés.

Because the national and international prestige of departments is coextensive with their scholarly progeny, universities invest considerable resources to support doctoral students in the departmental disciplines. These are prominent budget lines within the arts-and-sciences core. Doctoral students in the social sciences and humanities consume notoriously numerous years to complete their degrees.[13] Tuition, living expenses, and benefits all must be accounted for meanwhile, and unlike with undergraduate scholarship aid, the short-term costs of doctoral support are difficult to recoup through alumni contributions down the line. Nonetheless, top scholars demand that universities underwrite the cost of academic reproduction. The recruitment of good faculty in the present and the promise of famous students going forward require investment in doctoral training. So thoughtful administrators make generous but strategic investments in doctoral programs. Almost invariably the disciplinary departments get priority in the distribution of doctoral funding in the arts-and-sciences divisions of US research universities.[14]

Academic departments enjoy the privilege of self-governance. Their jurisdiction is limited to faculty selection and review, curriculum development, research, and instruction, but this purview includes the symbolic and technical cores of university life. Faculty jurisdiction over academic appointments and instruction in no way obliges them to actually carry out these tasks on their own. Growing legions of administrative and nontenured teaching staff do much of the work. But their formal authority distinguishes the Brahmins from the rest of the workers in the intramural caste system. At a fundamental level, academic administrators and instructors work at the pleasure of the tenured faculty.[15]

Abbott recognized an inherent tension of an academic labor system organized around encouraging scholarly research in disciplines. America's great universities enjoy general public respect as well as public and private subsidy on the promise that they are substantively useful, even while many faculty researchers work as hard as they can to avoid the study of real-world problems. As Abbott explained years ago, the measure and prestige of professional labor is the extent to which experts are able to deal with problems abstracted from the messiness of their empirical circumstances.[16] Just as the most privileged physicians are those who deal only with the medical malady (the brain tumor, the coronary blockage) and leave patients' bedpans and insurance troubles to subordinate workers, so too do the most privileged academic faculty work on puzzles that have largely been extracted from the exigencies of context. Work on problems that retain their integument of the real world, often called "applied research" by academics, is valued much more modestly by disciplinary elites than it is by the general public. Thus university leaders and fund-raisers perpetually face a conflict between creating ideal working conditions for star faculty in the disciplines while simultaneously assuring trustees, donors, funding agencies, and state legislatures that investment in research in abstractions is worthwhile for useful public return.

Not-Departments and the Disciplinary System

Not-departments are key mechanisms through which universities manage this tension. Table 3.1 offers a schematic comparison of departments and not-departments as organizational containers.

Even a brief consideration of the differences between the columns makes evident why not-departments are so appealing to academic managers. They can be brought into existence and nurtured to various stages of maturity with more tentative investment than departments require to be minimally viable. Without the obstacle of tenured faculty, not-departments also are easier to kill or allow to die. And unlike with academic departments that are ranked and rated by third-party status judges, not-departments are rarely subjected to scalar evaluation by outsiders. They can be called "excellent" or "nationally prominent" or "best" or "unique" without risk of contrary quantification in popular magazines. Their constitutional flexibility and relative exemption from rankings make not-departments exceptionally useful devices for managing appearances, and exploiting opportunities at the periphery of the arts-and-sciences core.

Table 3.1. Departments and Not-Departments Compared

	Departments	Not-Departments
Inputs	Faculty lines (tenure, non), doctoral funding, administrative budgets, space	Instructorships, partial lines, administrative budgets, space, gifts, endowments, grants (internal, external)
Production units	Topics, courses, degree programs (BA, MA, PhD), peer-reviewed scholarship	Language courses, degree courses (MA), scholarly support, events, public resources
Governance	Collegial self-governance	Varied
Success markers	Enrollments, faculty publication/fame, doctoral student placement, program rankings	Enrollments, faculty participation, external funding, events, attendance counts

Positioned between publics and disciplinary research, not-departments are ideal objects for fund-raising. Foundations with specifically defined portfolios, individual donors with particular passions, and government agencies with targeted requests for proposals all can be accommodated by not-departments without much tampering at the departmental core. This was precisely the intent of the area studies centers brought into being by Title VI. Their purpose was not to challenge the department/discipline structure but to augment and enrich it by encouraging scholarly engagement with real-world problems in particular places. The centers did not replace departments but were created alongside them. They were an added academic layer, funded by a deep-pocketed and prestigious third party—the federal government. The centers brought more resources to arts-and-sciences programs without obliging them to substantially change their core administration and governance.

Even while they enable universities to take in resources from their environments without disrupting disciplines, not-departments also contribute capacity to disciplinary enterprises. Appointees to director and associate director positions in not-departments add academic lines and personnel who can be deployed in the service of disciplinary activity. And because, as we will see below, their survival is dependent on the goodwill of departmental faculty, people who make their livings in not-departments have a constitutional incentive to cater to disciplinary faculty.

Whatever they are called—centers, institutes, forums, projects—they have densely populated the American academic landscape at least as long as disciplinary departments, although growth has been disproportionately tilted toward not-departments in the past few decades. Systematic archival work at our eight case universities makes this clear. Figure 3.1 provides a graphical depiction of the founding dates of units devoted to the study of world regions or regionally specified culture areas (for example, Oriental Studies) at the case universities.

Consonant with the historical narrative we provided earlier, departments were the default organizational unit for housing research on regions and regionally specific cultural traditions at the beginning of the twentieth century. Not-departments emerged as substantial alternatives for housing regional inquiry during the early Cold War decades, and then became the preponderant form for regionally focused activity by the end of the twentieth century.

Essential to the utility of not-departments in any intramural academic ecology is their strong legitimacy. They are completely naturalized components of research universities. This legitimacy is abetted by the great capacity they offer to entrepreneurial faculty.

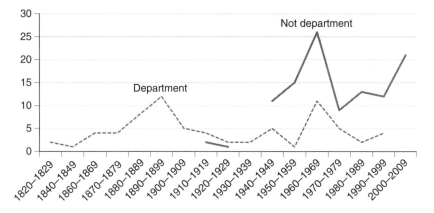

Figure 3.1. Founding years of academic units devoted to regional inquiry at eight case universities, 1820–2009.
Note: Based on original archival research by Jonathan Friedman and Mona Saghri, Social Science Research Council, 2014. Methodology and coding scheme are available upon request.

Although it can be exceedingly difficult to get one's departmental colleagues to go one way or another, as titular head of a not-department a faculty member can build whatever kingdom she pleases—as long as the requisite titles and real estate can be gotten from the provost and funding secured from within or beyond. Little wonder that academic managers routinely offer funding for centers and institutes to recruit or retain top researchers.

If the disciplinary system is virtually unbreakable, it is partly because of a plural organizational structure in which disciplinary departments are buffered and abetted by a thick ring of not-departments.[17] The things not-departments tend to lack—tenured appointments, independent doctoral training, and academic self-governance—make them categorically inferior in status to tenure-granting units and, we argue, ultimately dependent on them. But it is hard to imagine the American academic enterprise without them.[18]

The area studies centers funded by Title VI are the paradigmatic example of not-departments in post–World War II US universities. The configuration of academic inquiry by world regions is longstanding; however, the creation of government-funded research centers as official vehicles for regional inquiry was a specific joint venture of academic researchers, foundations, and multiple federal agencies during the Cold War.[19] From their first incarnations and into the present, Title VI–funded centers have had all the signal characteristics of not-departments. They are academic units typically without their own tenured faculty or doctoral students. They are specifically purposed with providing disciplinary researchers with basic tools (language training, research support) for pursuing scholarship, producing instruction and useful knowledge on world regions, and improving public awareness and understanding.

Because our fieldwork was directed specifically to the question of how regional studies take place in relation to social science disciplines, our interviews with center personnel, departmental faculty, and deans ideally equip us to investigate the relationships between departments and not-departments more generally. In what follows we listen to center leaders talk about all they do to support academic activity in the departments of the arts-and-sciences core, and how much they ultimately rely on departmental faculty to maintain their centers' reputations and even existence. We claim no unbiased accounting here. Our task is not to verify factually the statements of center leaders and other academic personnel, but to use them as insights into the structure of relationships between centers and departments generally. We find that these relations are deeply reciprocal but asymmetrically so.

At Their Service

The founding purpose of the area studies programs funded by Title VI was to provide practical support for scholarly inquiry on particular world regions. They were intended to be servants of academic researchers by providing language training, research travel, and focused academic inquiry. And in fact we found that the centers did much to facilitate scholarship. Center directors routinely touted these contributions. One Russia/Eurasia center director gave a specific example:

> [Name of student in Anthropology] wrote her dissertation on the statue farm outside of Budapest—this place where all the sort of Stalinist stuff was taken, sort of remainders. She did something on public monuments, which I am sure was a really interesting dissertation and we gave her a FLAS [Foreign Language and Area Studies Fellowship], maybe more than one. Of course she took Hungarian language here, and she took other classes.

The director of another Eastern European center at a wealthy private university spoke more generally of the material supports his program offered to students:

> We certainly have had PhD students [here] in the last five years who worked on this part of the world. And they'll come to events and sometimes we'll give them travel funding. We have quite a bit of student travel money. We spend about a $60,000 a year I think it is on graduate student travel. . . . And I don't know the exact

number [but] we do $15,000 or $20,000 on undergraduates. We also do undergraduate student internships [during the] summer. We have a small human rights program which last year did two undergraduate internships in Russia. So I would say that part of it is expanding. And in our endowment we have funds that are earmarked for student travel. We also do two PhD dissertation write-ups a year. Plus we have workspace for any PhD student at [the university] who is working on Russia and wants a desk here. Basically all they have to do is ask for it. So we have right now, I think desks for about eight.

As the acknowledgment sections of countless doctoral dissertations suggest, contributions such as these can matter a lot to scholarly progress.

Centers funded by Title VI also have a constitutional obligation to support "outreach"—to make knowledge about world regions available to educators and the general public. This is an important way in which area studies programs make good on the service missions of universities. We provide but one example here, from a center staff member at a Middle East center at a large public university, of a common refrain:

We get a lot of outreach requests. [For example, names a local public organization] has a constantly running lecture series and they have members soliciting, you know, giving them ideas. 'Oh, someone wants to hear about the war in Iraq. Do you have someone?' And so we'll find them a graduate student or a faculty member that will go over and do it and that's what [name of staff person] is going to start working on because [name of other staff person] has been doing that. . . . And for me it's tracking these people down and getting them visas and reimbursing their travel . . .

In doing such practical management, centers help universities make good on official commitments to serving public knowledge.[20]

Research support and public outreach are two explicit and therefore obvious roles of centers relative to the disciplinary departments, but centers make other, less official but no less important contributions to the organizational ecology of research universities. First, their very presence can be used as a recruitment tool in competitive faculty searches. A Russia/Eurasia center director at a different public university, himself a senior member of the sociology department there, volunteered such a case to our interviewer:

We can talk about the most recent hire. We have [name] who was hired in early 2000s and it was in part, she just surfaced in the top list, but we also made sure that she knew about this [center], and in part it's the attraction of [name of center] that enabled her to make the choice of this place over others. So I think some departments see us as an asset in recruiting their top choices. We are not going to tell them that you should choose this person because she does Poland. Rather she will choose to come to [this university] because it's an opportunity to work with [us].

Savvy departments know how to leverage centers as enticements for particular hires. The director of a South Asia center at a different public university provided this anecdote:

The other day [someone from] the computer science department came up to us and said there's a computer scientist they're trying to recruit who happens to be of Indian background, and he happened to be working on low-cost computers in developing areas. So we immediately put together a group of people to sit and chat [with] him.

Second, centers provide labor and letterhead to now elaborate processes of faculty review. These contributions are not trivial. As academic evaluation becomes more formally meritocratic it requires ever more formal evaluation. Promotion and tenure files must be fatter than ever to survive the review gauntlet, with more ceremony to verify worth.[21] Center personnel routinely lend their attention and the imprimatur of their offices to this evaluation regime. As the chair of the political science department of a top-ranked public research university explained:

When we constitute a search committee in the first place, there must be representation from the studies center, someone who is in the center and not a member of the department. So just to begin with they are represented in that way . . . it guarantees that there is at least voice and maybe tremendous influence wielded by the studies center in whom we decide to offer a position to. If this involves tenure or if we are reviewing for tenure somebody on the inside who has a coordinated appointment with the studies center then we get their advice on whom we should ask for outside letters for review. We ask them to prepare a letter of evaluation that becomes the part of the formal process. So there is involvement of that sort, which is not constant, but at very serious junctures there is very considerable representation.

Even when, as we will see below, center input on faculty appointments is clearly circumscribed, center personnel contribute labor to the machinery of faculty evaluation. This work was a common theme of our interviews with center directors, as, for example, in the words of the faculty director of the Middle East studies center at the same public university:

> If people have played a role, even if not the biggest role, but they have done something for our students or participated in outreach and so on, I write a letter on their behalf to the chair of their department and say, 'At this key point Professor X came through and [we] relied on his or her knowledge of this particular thing he or she does, and it was important and the graduate students benefited and the community saw that.' And I think what that does is it makes people feel like this is yet another good reason for us to keep an individual they want to keep already. Now if they don't want to keep the person I don't think that's going to make or break, or they are going to change their view of a tenure decision, but if they want the person it's a nice extra bonus and it's taken seriously. Otherwise people wouldn't keep asking me. Now that I think about it I can think of five in the last three years, so actually I do that quite a lot.

Third, relative to the social science departments of economics, sociology, and political science at the universities we studied, it appears that regional studies programs offer coverage to that great bane of academic research faculty: the master's degree. Different from the undergraduates whose enrollments are essential to the distribution of faculty lines, and from the doctoral students whose presence is essential to faculty reproduction and prestige, masters students are primarily revenue streams and public relations for arts-and-sciences divisions. Master's students typically seek degrees specifically for professional enhancement. Their interest in academic fields is "applied" almost by definition, and they typically do not stay long enough to develop scholarly portfolios that might substantially serve the ambitions of departmental faculty. So it did not surprise us to learn that of the twenty-four social science departments that were part of our study at eight premier US research universities, only seven had terminal master's programs. By contrast, master's programs are fairly common features of Title VI centers. Of the twenty-four centers we studied on these same eight campuses, thirteen supported terminal master's. This too was unsurprising. The mandates of Title VI–funded centers make their work "applied" as well. Yet another way in which regional studies programs enable arts-and-sciences divisions to connect with larger publics, then, is by providing nonacademic professionals with opportunities for cognate study on world regions.

Overall, centers convey resources into the arts-and-sciences cores of universities that disciplinary departments would be hard pressed to bring in on their own. To the extent that these resources are available to departmental faculty, the centers are welcome neighbors. As a staff member at a Middle East studies center put it:

> People generally seem to like us, and like to hear from us and they know who we are. Generally if I call one of those departments we work with frequently, they know who I am and I know who they are, and I've been here long enough now that I pretty much know everyone that we go back and forth with. And primarily what I do is I give them money [laughs]. Everyone likes to hear from me, because it generally means we're giving them some money for some program or course or visiting scholar that they're doing.

At Their Pleasure

By no means does good-neighbor status imply equality. Because they are not departments, area studies centers participate only very partially in the selection and appointment of disciplinary faculty. In addition, centers must rely on disciplinary departments to provide the academic coursework essential to their own instructional programs.

The centers we studied typically have budgets to hire adjunct instructors, or in the best cases contract lines for multiple-year appointments. But only rarely do they have tenure-track positions of their own. "The center itself will never have the kind of money to make faculty, I mean to hire actual faculty," explained one associate director, "We can hire more adjuncts." "We as the center here don't have any significant leverage on the [departments'] policies in terms of hiring, and also on course offerings," said a Middle East center director. Center directors cited this lack of ability to hire as their largest administrative constraint. "The most important thing are the faculty who are appointed or recruited to the university," explained one center director, who went on to note that Title VI "has next to nothing to do with that."

Consistent with Abbott's theory of faculty allocation, our respondents routinely reminded us that departments received faculty lines at least partly on the basis of undergraduate enrollments, and that departments had almost complete control over who was hired into those positions. Those two facts together mean that centers are constitutionally reliant on departments to get their own work done. As one Russia/Eurasia center director (who is himself in a faculty appointment) put it bluntly: "SCH, it's student credit hours . . . the beans that are counted at this university are how many student credit semester credit hours are charged to [Russia/Eurasia] studies." "We get all happy when we hit triple digits," he said at another moment. "In the first year we were like 'look we hit a 100 [students] this year, that's so great.'" An associate director at a Middle East center at a different university said:

> You've got departments like poli-sci and sociology, and history that have these huge you know 1000-enrollment core courses that all undergraduates have to take, and therefore those departments get a lot of the money. Whereas departments like NES or Slovak don't have those really huge core courses and I think, the finances really shape the ways some departments are treated.

When faculty lines are allocated to academic departments, center personnel typically are peripheral to decision making. One senior international officer described her relationships between area studies centers and the departments as:

> . . . complicated, because none of us—area studies or center for international studies—have faculty. All faculty are faculty in departments, and departmental autonomy is jealously guarded. So the idea that any interdisciplinary unit can affect hiring is quite unlikely.

There is only so much center personnel can do to influence faculty affairs. "The departments have a lot of power and they really have autonomy," this officer said later on. "So we can only sort of cajole. We can't really coerce."

Center directors are well aware of this state of affairs. "I wish that we had a formal voice in campus-wide appointments in the region . . . related areas, and we don't," said one director of a Middle East center. "We're a center, we're not a department. . . . My sense is that our role, the center's role in making those hires, is as a consulting one," said an associate director elsewhere. This power difference shapes pretty much everything center personnel do, as the associate director of a Middle East studies center at a prestigious private university explained:

> I think it is always difficult to sort of navigate between the desires of each department. . . . The desires of the centers are always met with the demands of other departments. So if the center feels that there is a need for a language professor or somebody who's trained . . . they sort of have to work together with the demands of other departments that might want professors in other fields,

or they are reliant on their budgets, on their priorities, on different opinions within each department, on the ways in which departments hire. Some departments hire by regions, some departments hire by disciplines, some departments hire by needs. They sort of have to sometimes tailor their demands to what the departments have in mind. Because the center doesn't hire independently.

Even in the relatively rare instances when centers do contribute partial funding for faculty appointments, their influence on outcomes is subordinate to departmental judgments. Consider, for example, this exchange between our interviewer and the faculty director of a South Asia center at a large public research university. At the time of the interview, the university had a special emphasis on international affairs that enabled a few regional studies programs to contribute 50 percent of tenure-line appointments to do joint hires with departments:

INTERVIEWER: How much power do you have over a department, such as economics, for example, even if you have a 50/50 position, they ultimately at the end of the day have to approve that person I assume, and if they don't feel that the person is—
DIRECTOR: 50/50 is 50/50.
INTERVIEWER: Really?
DIRECTOR: Both departments have to approve.
INTERVIEWER: Hmm-mm.
DIRECTOR: Can they veto them? Yes. A concrete example last year is a geography position where the first person was a joint position, meaning the budget lines are split between two departments [sic].
INTERVIEWER: The first person decided not to take the job, and instead of going to the second person who would have been equally valuable for us as someone who worked on Bangladesh, the Geography department unilaterally decided that they didn't want to hire that person. And it just ended there. So the committee had made its recommendations. If not "A" then "B," if not "B" then "C," and the chair decided that he wasn't going to go forward with that. No reason given. Nothing could be done. It just ended there.
INTERVIEWER: Yeah, OK.
DIRECTOR: So how much power do you have? It's like moral suasion, right, it's like the way that [the] Federal Reserve tries to tell banks not to lend money to bad people.

The preponderance of our interviews indicates that even this degree of influence over hires is exceptional, because most regional studies centers do not have independent capacity to make academic appointments. "[T]he thing about the Institute here, and indeed most of the centers I suspect that you have encountered, is that they don't have the power to make academic appointments," said a Latin American studies center director. He was right. The director of a Middle East studies center said that his is a university

> . . . in which the real cornerstones of the institution are departments, and departments are understood in disciplinary terms. And even when those disciplines have got an area studies title attached to them, I mean, really it's that disciplinary function that is important rather than the area studies function.

In this joint interview, the associate director of the same center weighed in:

> I think that inevitably, at almost any institution, departmental, not disciplinary, but just departmental structures win out. Because departments have the authority to teach classes and hire personnel. And Middle East centers or area studies centers may or may not grant degrees. . . . But even in the case when centers grant degrees, they do not have the authority to teach a single class unless a department agrees to offer it. I mean every single class. . . . Every class has to be vetted by a department and offered through a department. And departments have the ability to hire faculty, so whatever agenda the centers may have about what they want to teach or who they want to hire, those things have ultimately to be fit in to the self-image of departments.

Center directors generally supported the disciplinary structure of universities, even if they wished they had more power within it. "My feeling is that a department is ideally a discipline," said the director quoted above, "ideally, a department represents some kind of disciplinary configuration." The senior international officer at the same university said:

> It's a very difficult problem in the sense that to build area studies, you really need social science people, but social science disciplines don't hire that way. So, all we can do is work indirectly, but . . . I am myself a social scientist and a member of a department and I certainly don't want area studies centers telling us who we should hire. So I am sympathetic to both sides of it . . . the other South

Asianists within anthropology and I are always scheming about how we can get more South Asianists, but we have to get them past the whole faculty, so it is a tricky problem . . . we are constantly scheming. There's no question about that [laughs].

Desperately Seeking

"The departmental structure of this university really does bite back at us a little bit," said the director just quoted, since all affiliated faculty have to do their own service in their departments, and "that actually takes up quite a chunk of people's time." One consequence of this organization of human resources is that centers are chronically reliant on departments to fill out center programming. One Middle East studies center administrator summed it succinctly: "We have courses but no faculty." An assistant director elsewhere said, "I just want to make sure that we are clear, the center itself doesn't offer a lot of courses. We rely on the faculty throughout the university to offer the courses." This fact creates several chronic problems for centers, not the least of which is scheduling. A faculty director of a Russia/Eurasia center at yet another school explained:

> We don't control what's offered in departments. We just can't. There is nothing we can do. Every single year we do our exit polls, our questionnaires for our graduating MA students. Every year they say, "The number one problem is everything is scheduled at the same time. Can't you get this together?" And the answer is we can't. We're an interdisciplinary program with dozens and dozens of schools and departments. Even organizing it under the best of the circumstances would be difficult, but with this situation, I mean, what can we do, we can't tell . . . because those administrators at the very last minute are slotting things into classes and they can't possibly worry about whether it conflicts with some other course in History that we happen to care about, if they're in Poli-Sci or what have you.

The director of the South Asia program at the same university said:

> One of those things that we are constantly having to work on is freeing up the time of our colleagues to offer courses for us, because their fundamental responsibilities are to the department, and not to the South Asian program. We have to badger and plead, till we have our core courses and then options and electives covered . . . [because faculty's] primary responsibilities for promotion and tenure and for teaching are still in departments.

She said elsewhere, "The first thing I learned . . . [in this] job is humility. You go . . . to colleagues and say, 'Please, please, please teach a course. It's actually for the good of the university.'"

Regardless of their particular accomplishments, center personnel are ultimately dependent on the goodwill and cooperation of particular people and relationships. When asked about the relationships between centers and social science departments at the school we call UWest, an associate dean for international programs replied:

SIO: I think a lot of the difference depends on just the faculty incumbents in those departments at any particular time. You know, if a center has faculty in those disciplines usually there is more involvement. Not always, you know if a faculty member just doesn't want to get involved in those sorts of things then you know you are kind of out of luck.

INTERVIEWER: So it sounds like it's largely individuals and their personalities across the board, both the directors and the individuals in the departments.

SIO: I think to a large degree it is. I don't think you can underplay that idiosyncratic nature of the personalities. The centers can do something if they are strategic in their funding opportunities for faculty and also are somewhat strategic in the way they put strings on them and say, we really are interested in supporting the people who are involved. That does play a role certainly in pulling in these faculty to do work. But I have to be honest there are certain faculty who just don't want to be involved.

Interviews with center personnel left little question that their relationships with departmental faculty were not coequal. The director of the Middle East center at UWest was blunt about this. While he seemed proud of his center's capacity to enlist faculty involvement, he was careful to note their asymmetry:

All of these faculty benefit from the center's resources, i.e., they get grants from the center, they use the center's physical space, they use money from the center and research assistance from the center through the conferences—none of them are accountable to the center because none of them report to me.

Later on he recounted one consequence of this arrangement:

We have a Middle East major that does not belong to any department . . . I chair that major. In my [role as] chair of the center, I automatically chair [the major]. Now this major used to have five or six students before September 11th; now it has 40 or something like that. . . . This is great. Well, yes and no. Why? Because this is a major with no budget, with no funding, and with no faculty. And you can say, "Yes that's great because the students have to take courses in political science, in history, in anthropology." That's also very good, except that it's here exactly the issue of accountability, where I am vulnerable to who among my faculty is doing what at that given semester, and whether indeed they are going to be on sabbatical, on leave, or teaching something else than what is really needed to fulfill that thing.

In light of the basic power imbalance, savvy directors figure out how to tie their fates to programs with strong departmental players, as in the words of this Slavic studies program director at a different public university:

History just got—our new president is trying to do this going-from-good-to-great thing about some of our departments that are kind of mid-ranked nationally now to try to make them top 10 percent ranked. And History was the first one chosen by our new president and given a grant of . . . 1.6 or 1.7 million [dollars] to infuse it with new faculty, new courses, new technology over the course of the next year or so. That's good for us as well because a lot of . . . , we have four dedicated faculty members who do courses in [Russia/Eurasian] history, so that's good news for us. And that's kind of what we rely on. We rely on these departments internally to maintain enough of a healthy structure so that we can in a sense use them as zero-term appointments in our center. That's where it's really important. And here again my role as Chair/Director is a little bit advantageous rather than just being a Director. Because what I need to do is get to whoever is Chair when a new hire comes along. So I say "Oh you are making a new hire in Anthro? Wouldn't it be great if this person did Central Asia? Wouldn't it be great if this person did Siberia?" Something like that. That is my role of playing advocate.

Not-Departments and Academic Identities

An ecology of academic units structured on the binary of departments and not-departments has implications for the identities of academic professionals. Recent sociology makes clear how much identity matters as an incentive for scholarship in the humanities and social sciences. Scholars define themselves intellectually, and even morally, on the basis of how they evaluate the work of others.[22] Where in the academic system one works shapes the scholarship one does.[23] We also know that competition among departments and disciplines for recognition and students is a primary dimension of academic politics at the arts-and-sciences cores of US research universities.[24] Less appreciated by prior observers, however, are the wide variety of identities available to academic workers in US universities and the reciprocal implications of this variety with academic politics.

In a positive sense, the proliferation of not-departments around the disciplinary core creates opportunity for some academics to enjoy the flexibility of claiming multiple academic identities simultaneously. Several center directors who also were tenured faculty members suggested the enlarged political capacity their joint roles gave them. Take the instance of a Russia/Eurasia center director who simultaneously held appointments in a center and a department. His appointment to the center directorship replaced a prior incumbent who did not have the same titles:

> It just changed . . . from the position of leveraging funding, leveraging courses. It really helps in my curricular decisions when I go to the dean with questions like, 'We would like to offer Uzbek on a two-year sequence, could we do this?' I can go in as Chair to ask about the curricular benefits of that, and then go in as Director to help talk about the funding of this. So it's kind of nice to be able to do the two sides of it.

The comment of a faculty director of a Middle East center at a different university clarified one distinction between the capacities of his two titles. "I get to play a role in [hiring] as much as I am faculty in one of the departments. But as the center director? Unfortunately, no."

As institutional theorists have long understood, having a variety of possible identities creates conditions for multiple forms of action by the same people.[25] But it also can engender ambiguous identities and identity conflict. One associate director of Middle East studies did not sound as if she was bragging when she said, "I have like eight different titles. I literally have eight different titles." The words of a faculty director of a Latin American center at a private university suggested a strong difference between the capacities of a center director and those of faculty at the departmental core:

> Departments here are not even baronies, I mean, they are sort of hordes of prima donnas. There are state universities where a provost or dean can mandate stuff. . . . The spirit here is intellectual freedom and that means intellectual freedom for a department to dig its own grave, intellectual freedom for faculty to offer whatever courses they feel like, which means that if someone who is a

Latin Americanist wants to start giving courses on Japan or on the US Congress, that's what they want to do. I like that very, very much but—but it means that any fantasy of sort of a sovereign directive to rebuild area studies is just a fantasy.

One of his colleagues, a faculty member who also was associate director of that university's Middle East studies center, provided a different elaboration:

Centers do not hire people. I wasn't hired by the center, I was hired by [my department]. You [referring to another colleague in the joint interview] weren't hired by the center, you were hired by [the department], and so, even if we have strong attachments to the center, which we do, and see the center as having its own identity and its own agenda in a certain way, inevitably, I'm also involved in and concerned with the agendas of the department into which I was hired and where I do also teach and vote. So centers have that funny kind of overlapping identity thing always. I don't know that there is any way to escape that ever. Unless you made centers into departments, which would have problems of its own.

There is little doubt that center affiliations by themselves provide less prominent identities among players at the arts-and-sciences core. Consider for example how a sociology chair described the relationship between his department and the centers we came to interview him about:

When I write an annual report or when I prepare a fact sheet that describes our department and what we do, the area centers are listed, are kind of included in our reference to our connections to the [international school] but it's not viewed as a real significant component of our programs or our success. . . . When I first got your letter, I didn't even, I guess really knew there was a center for Middle East . . . I knew about the South Asian because of [names of faculty] . . . but I didn't know about the Russia/Europe. I didn't even know about it.

Even while the steady accretion of not-departments creates more titles and niches for academic professionals, faculty appointments in departments retain their privilege in the academic status system.

CHAPTER 4

Stone Soup

Academic life is a complicated collage of team activity. No one can produce a curriculum, run a program, mentor students, or produce good scholarship entirely on their own. Getting academic work done means cooperating with many others in many ways, simultaneously. One reason for the reputation of professors as absent-minded is that they manage participation on so many teams at the same time.

Some of these teams are distributed widely across physical space and continue over long periods—for example, the scholarly professional associations whose annual meetings structure faculty calendars as surely as semesters and summer breaks. Others are less formal but no less important for academic production: the enduring relationships among scholars and students who may live and work at great distances from each other even while they comprise the "invisible colleges" through which so much scholarship is produced, critiqued, and improved.[1]

Then there are the local intramural teams whose activities fill the daily lives of faculty, staff, and students on particular university campuses. We sketched the basic mechanics of two categories of such teams in Chapter 3. Academic departments are perhaps the most privileged teams in university organization. They have a high degree of autonomy and their most powerful members enjoy lifetime tenure. There are many other formal structures for academic teamwork that fall into the category of not-departments, and although they lack the durability and prestige of the department form, their assets of flexibility and legitimacy make them perennially popular. Yet departments and not-departments hardly exhaust the stock of organizing strategies available to academic workers in the contemporary US academy. A great deal of activity takes place between and among departments and not-departments, not just within them. Any complete account of academic production must include attention to cross-unit endeavor.

That endeavor does not just happen. Any act of cooperation entails appraisals of cost and benefit by participating parties, negotiation, and some sort of governance system to ensure the consistent enforcement of norms and rules.[2] Cooperation also entails templates and routines that people can use to make sense of what they are doing with one another. This is what sociologist Elisabeth Clemens calls "the 'how' of organization"—shared understandings which guide people as they negotiate their relationships.[3] The cooperation of interdisciplinary scholarship requires additional scaffolding.[4] Disparate ways of seeing, and making knowledge about, the world create conditions ripe for misunderstanding. Throw in the great extent to which professional identities are intertwined with the mechanics of doing scholarship, and it is remarkable that interdisciplinary endeavor happens at all.

Yet directors of area studies centers repeatedly emphasized how much of their work was devoted to working cooperatively, both with other centers and with academic departments. "We do a lot of co-sponsoring of things," a Latin America center director said, "our center doesn't have a very big budget and so virtually everything that we promote or initiate ourselves works on a sort of stone soup principle where we get multiple co-sponsorships." An associate director of the Russia/Eurasia center at the same university said:

> We've taken the stone soup approach to things. Someone conceives of an idea; we decide we are going to run with it, we say "okay this is what we can do" . . . looking at places on campus and off for support. And we can cobble together enough to do some really exciting events.

The metaphor took some of us to childhood memories, and others to Wikipedia, to recall a famous folk tale in which a group of hungry travelers enters a village bearing only an empty pot. To entice the villagers to feed them, the travelers fill their pot with water from a nearby stream, add a stone, and begin to heat it over a fire. When locals make inquiries on their doings, the travelers reply that they are making stone soup: a delicious recipe that would be much enhanced with only a few additional ingredients. One by one, the locals contribute an ingredient to the pot until it ultimately makes a hearty meal.

The story illustrates an important aspect of social action. Modest individual investments can accumulate to substantial collective rewards. We agree that stone soup is a good metaphor for how people in not-departments especially, but also academic entrepreneurs more generally, pursue survival and prestige for their endeavors in the US academic world. For the people who run area studies centers, Title VI funds provide money and status that can be leveraged to build joint ventures. The modest funding and third-party endorsement centers receive through Title VI grants are akin to the folktale's pot and stone. They are assets that can be leveraged in negotiations with other players. The Title VI seal of approval reduces uncertainty for collaborators, who may make a variety of contributions to a joint venture: money, of course, but also mailing lists, faculty and student attention, administrative time, physical facilities, and the prestige of their association.

Our interviews enable us to depict this phenomenon richly, and thereby contribute to recent sociological considerations of interdisciplinarity in the US academy. Specifically, we can investigate in some detail Jerry Jacobs' recent assertion that interdisciplinary centers and institutes facilitate cross-specialty collaboration. Sharply countering many recent calls for restructuring the US academy along interdisciplinary lines, Jacobs suggests that a constantly thickening web of extra-departmental research units—our not-departments—sustain a good deal of cross-disciplinary fertilization within the current academic regime.[5] Our inquiry strongly supports this assertion.

In the following sections we listen closely to center directors, showing how they cooperate with other parties to burnish their centers' as well as their personal identities while getting things done. Doing so allows us to offer a more general insight into the production of academic work. That work is complexly distributed, requiring the coordination of many resources and voices across organizational space and varying stretches of time. Exploiting the plural department/not-department structure of US universities, canny players in the American academic field have developed highly productive routines for pursuing joint ventures. The master routine is co-sponsorship, and it takes many forms. We call it stone soup.

Co-sponsorship

Co-sponsorship is the meat and potatoes of center directors' work. Directors both initiate and respond to requests for co-sponsorship, contributing often modest, short-term resources but occasionally investing in long-term collaboration. Directors enter co-sponsorships with departments and other centers to host the myriad lectures, performances, exhibits, and conferences that swell the calendars of great universities. At least as center directors tell it (and they are admittedly a biased source—more on this later), a good deal of academic activity would simply not take place were it not for co-sponsorship.

Directors often operate with very modest material assets, and their job is to make those assets do as much as possible. "In the big scheme of things it's not a large sum of money, we have probably $250,000 per year, but it is incredible what can be done with this money to raise awareness of the region," said one Russia/Eurasia center director. When the job is done well, a center has visibility disproportionate to its budget. One Middle East director said that his is "a vaporous organization . . . theoretically we are everywhere, practically we occupy a fairly small space." "We do it in spades," he later said of co-sponsorship:

> In terms of the day-to-day labor and energy of the center . . . we almost always say yes to things like co-sponsoring, advertising, getting the word out, and it's one of those things that's never sort of captured in terms of when we describe what we do either within the university or to organizations like the [US Department of Education]. I don't think that there is really any way to capture the amount of time you spend producing advertisements, flyers, posters, sending emails . . . in terms of co-sponsoring even without money, I think we still put a lot of effort into it, and that counts for something.

"Every lecture on our calendar has co-sponsorship," said an associate director of a Middle East center elsewhere:

> You won't find an activity that we don't share the costs. . . . Usually we approach the department that is relevant to the topic or to the speaker, or they approach us. . . . And our faculty, if they have projects that they need funding for, they come to us. They usually go to other sources of funding too, so almost everything is co-sponsored. Even with the medical center we're co-sponsoring an event on medical history . . . it's a very prestigious event . . . it's going to be about a physician, he discovered treatments for cancer and all this other stuff back in 11th century, and he was Muslim. And then we'll have a public lecture also co-sponsored by them, and the venue will be in the medical center.

Event co-sponsorships leverage material assets but also prestige.[6] The latter is sometimes the primary feature of the contribution. One staff member who counted fifty-six co-sponsorships during a recent academic year said, "We can co-sponsor in a way where sometimes people will just want to use our name to get their event credibility." Another director elsewhere said:

> The mechanism for getting other people to recognize the significance of something is saying, "Would you co-sponsor?" And people

do that, especially if they are not having to put huge amounts of money on the table. Generally speaking, people take a look at it and if it looks interesting they'll say, "Yeah, sure we'll co-sponsor it."

The Latin America center director who invoked the stone-soup metaphor also said, "We are often approached by people asking for small co-sponsorships, which is about the most we can give, and so we get involved as co-sponsors of many, many events." A South Asia center director made clear that finding funds is only part of the incentive. Doing more with what one has is part of it too. "It's not that we cannot begin something because we don't have funds; it's more like we get the seed money to start something and then we go out and get more . . . and then we look for more money because we want to take it further."

Building relationships over time is important for much of this activity, as the Middle East center associate director who was proud of her medical school collaboration said. "Really, the way to cultivate these kind of contacts, you can't do a cold call. It's just not going to work." As she told it, the center's relationship with the medical school began decades ago, when the university hospital treated Afghani refugees from the Soviet occupation for free. Over the years, the medical school maintained an interest in Afghanistan and donated medical books and supplies to the region, with the Middle East center's help:

> They have all these extra medical books, all these extra supplies, and they just throw them away. And they have nothing in Afghanistan—they need everything. . . . It's surprisingly difficult to find a way to get the stuff there. . . . We didn't give up though, we invited the Afghan ambassador to come to [the university] and give a lecture and also to get him to be on our side and to use his connections in Afghanistan and so he's connected us with some groups who think they are going to be able to help us. And because of that we form relationships.

The director of a South Asia center made clear that supporting faculty travel was one way his center sought to build these relationships:

> [Travel funding] is a regular activity [that] we do. We are often able to fund [faculty] to a substantial extent of what they need, and we try to make them remember that they owe us one [associate director in joint interview laughs]. This is about relationships, and it is about various forms of exchange that makes a center like this function. So, we have a few things that we can offer, and then we'll turn to them and say give us something back by doing something for us. . . . It's not a market relationship. It's a barter relationship. A pre-modern form of interaction.

Experienced directors recognize that small investments can bring nontrivial returns over time. "Sometimes it is amazing," this South Asianist's associate director said elsewhere in the joint interview:

> Sometimes a very small amount of money, like $1000, $2000 towards a conference that they are having over in . . . the law school or something . . . will create the kind of political goodwill that [my colleague was] speaking of and this is one of the most if not *the* most important thing that we do is to establish these networks. And not only keep up the goodwill but be doing the work, by bringing in the South Asianists in various capacities.

Not having prior relationships to draw on can be a handicap of new directors. One who was new to his position at the time of our interview said:

> I came on as Director two months ago in the middle of the academic year, so frankly I haven't been able to build up much of those, just, informal relationships that—it's something that—that is going to happen and it's definitely sort of the type of network that makes this possible, rather than any sort of formal structure.

Center personnel seemed to be especially proud of programming they supported that, in their estimation, might not have happened otherwise. The director of a Middle East center at a public research university mentioned lecture and visitor programming:

> Now sponsoring guest speakers, visiting scholars—we actually do that. The departments don't do it. No department has a lecture series in Middle Eastern studies. No department even has a single lecture on Middle Eastern studies in which we are not the co-sponsor. So basically what happens is this; we are the sponsors of all of the lectures. We are the sponsors of all of the conferences. We are the sponsor of all visiting scholars. We do Middle Eastern Studies regardless of their department. If and when in the rare case that the department has done something on its own, then normally they would still come to us for co-sponsorship either because they need money, or they need publicity.

Because Title VI funds are explicitly intended to support regional and language instruction, directors spend a good deal of effort encouraging faculty to offer courses relative to their center's mission. This can be done with carrots to entice departmental faculty to offer courses, as an administrator for a Middle East Studies center said:

> We just try to remain as vibrant as we can and keep on with trying to find those interdisciplinary courses that we can cross-list. . . .

We keep on giving course development money to our affiliated faculty so they can . . . like for instance [name of faculty member] in the government department, we gave him some . . . Title VI money to go to the Egyptian elections. Now we have a course on Egyptian politics.

Directors also get relevant courses on the books by contributing to the cost of adjunct instructors. As one associate director who wanted some specific language instruction explained:

We were able to hire somebody because we chipped into the pot from our endowment and now from our grant, but for the first year from our endowment, and [also for] other languages and courses, so it's really helped us to have some leverage in getting and seeding positions to fit our agenda, what we want to see happen on campus.

"This we found extremely productive actually," one director said of the strategy of jointly paying for instructors, "because by the time a department gets used to a person we find out it costs us less and less because they are willing to put in that money into the course."

One of the most important forms of co-sponsorship is joint support of tenure-line appointments. Because they are not departments, centers generally are unable to make tenure-line appointments on their own. However, deans and provosts sometimes allow and even encourage shared tenure-line appointments between centers and departments. Because regionally expert faculty are essential to the work of area studies centers, and because tenure-line appointments in academic departments signal high prestige, directors pay a good deal of attention to how, where, and by whom tenure-line appointments are made.

Our respondents talked quite a bit about seeding ground for potential hiring and negotiating with other parties to grow that potential over time. One senior international officer described a recent case in which "a bunch of the South Asianists got together and decided that they would like to offer a job" to a historian and

. . . were able to get Middle East, South Asia . . . Anthro, History and so they—we were able . . . to form a kind of coalition and go both to the Provost and to the History department which would ultimately have to make the offer and to get a kind of enthusiasm and agreement. And there was an offer and it did work.

Similarly, a Middle East director explained that his center saw a need for an anthropologist with regional expertise, even though it "was not a priority" in the Anthropology department. So the center staff went to the department as well as to the dean and offered to pay for a quarter of a junior faculty member's salary for the first three years:

> So we got this agreement from them, they approved that . . . they found someone . . . so we funded her for 25 percent of her first cycle and then we reduced it. Now we're paying annually about 11 or 12 percent of that person's salary . . . So that's one way to leverage the money.

Giving a second example, the same director reported that Slavic and Middle East centers each agreed to pay 25 percent of a Central Asian historian position on the condition that the umbrella academic unit would cover the remaining half.

> This person will be funded, and after four years, the position will be adopted by the History department. So in four years we will have a Central Asian historian position institutionalized in [the university's] department of History. So that's what we are influencing.

"The term that we are using is that we are stretching the Title VI money," this director put it succinctly, "combine it with institutional funding, and that's how we pursue our objectives of the Middle East studies program." Stretching can take the form of deploying standing relationships and making pitches within the framework of senior administrators' priorities. "We are trying to leverage one search into two or three appointments," explained one director as he and the associate director discussed their efforts to build capacity on the center's target region.

> DIRECTOR: The [search] committee commissioned me . . . to talk to the Provost so that we can get an appointment with him to proselytize for this vision that we have of multiple appointments and not just one. We've already got the Vice President.
> ASSOCIATE: We are trying to get a two-for-one. . . . A three-for-one.
> DIRECTOR: You want the truth? We are looking for a four! . . . [laughs]. We're very ambitious.

The director of a South Asia center elsewhere said:

> This is the politics of this job, which is that you are trying to negotiate for positions. You are trying to work with deans, get them to put pressure on department chairs. You try and develop relationships with department chairs so that they think this is a good and interesting thing to be doing. You collaborate as much as possible through co-sponsorships with other centers because you are building up credits with them, which then you will be able to call in later on down the line.

Center directors and international officers sometimes made pre-
cise calculations about what proportions of faculty lines they would
cover and for how long, offering anywhere from a few thousand dollars to half of a salary and fringe benefits to motivate departments to
hire in particular areas. One Russia/Eurasia center director said, "we
set aside in our grant one-half of an academic salary basically for one
semester to bring someone over, hoping that the other, the sponsor-
ing department, would contribute another half." The ultimate goal
may be to get the departments to support the lines on their own,
in a process that may play out over very long periods of time—even
a generation or more. One senior international officer told us she
had two fifty-percent lines that she can use to encourage departments
to hire someone doing human rights and environmental work. If a
department accepts one of the fifty-percent lines, she explains, they
have "cut a deal" to essentially provide a full extra faculty member,
without that line counting against the quota of full-time appointments the department is allotted:

> And the money comes from the Provost's office, so they only have
> to pay half and the Dean isn't counting that person against their
> quota. And then eventually you hope the Dean will forget about
> it and then twenty, thirty, forty years and then that would be a
> permanent addition to the faculty.

Center participation in joint tenure-line hires is an important caveat to our arguments in the previous chapter. Tenure-line appointments are departmental affairs, and department faculty typically have
the upper hand in tenure-line appointment and review decisions.
Yet the routine of joint appointments does provide not-departments
with some influence over the ongoing evolution of faculty at the arts-
and-sciences core. Bargaining from the position of a center rather
than a department gives center directors weaker hands in the game,
but they can be at the table nevertheless. Savvy directors realize this
opportunity and play their cards with care.

Directors have many incentives to co-sponsor. Some are financial.
Often working with modest funds, directors do what they can to
make the funds go as far as they can. One Middle East center associate director admitted that because they had no independent endowment to cover the cost of operations, his unit was "dependent on
the good graces of the university." He explained, "it is one of those
things where there [are] no earmarked funds that are set aside for us.
We have to go every year and ask people for money." Other incentives
are regulatory. The official purpose of Title VI grants is to encourage
diffuse training, scholarship, and community outreach throughout

recipient institutions. Centers are obliged to demonstrate their collaborative activities every time they apply for government funding.

Still other incentives are reputational. A Middle East center administrator was clearly proud of her own work, but also competitive with other units on campus, when she told us, "I think we are the most vibrant. I know we are. But the South Asia institute is getting up there for sure, and doing things and spinning around and dancing with partners." We suspect that pride and competitiveness in collaboration come from the fact that centers are *not* departments, and so the things about which departments might boast—numbers of majors, the placement of graduates, national rankings—typically are not available ambitions for center personnel. The activities more directly within centers' purview provide a firmer basis for professional identity.

Whatever the combination of incentives for any particular center staff member, there is no doubt that co-sponsorship is an essential part of the job. As one put it:

> The point never to lose is that Title VI is foundational for everything that we do, and it's in fact so cost effective because it enables us to leverage way more university resources on this subject than would ever be offered by university priorities alone.

ॐ

Our research purview was defined by area studies centers and so in empirical terms we can speak only about them. Yet our respondents often indicated that the stone-soup routines described here were characteristic of how work got done throughout their universities. One Middle East studies associate director said, "It's a very capitalistic system we have here, it's like, 'Hey, great, if you can survive, go for it. Do what you need to do.' So you have the freedom to shape yourself. But everything you get, you have to get, you have to procure." Another said:

> All of our centers . . . are entrepreneurial by design. You cannot function around here unless you are a go-getter. So we are all. I mean you're either sort of Darwinian in a way, you know, if you don't learn to go out there and put things together on your own then you sit back and things don't happen. But everyone seems to make things happen.

"Capitalistic," "entrepreneurial," and "around here" were used with sufficient frequency in our interviews to suggest that respondents were describing features of academic life not peculiar to any one or two universities. Another common term was "bottom up." As one economics chair put it:

> This is just the way that things work, and it's also, I think our great strength actually is it's extremely decentralized and bottom up. So there is a huge amount of international activity but it's by and large not responding to centralized mandates and resources, but faculty members getting excited and doing things and getting the resources themselves, and I think that's a much healthier environment.

Different Soups

The basic recipe for stone soup is consistent across all the campuses we studied. We would expect this. Public events, college courses, faculty hires, and the department and not-department structures through which these activities are produced all are university staples. An organization would not be a research university if it did not have all those things.[7] Yet there also is a great variety of academic flavor across campuses. Schools differ substantially in resources, managerial structure, and cultural character. They have distinctive reputations. Stone soup allows and accounts for this variety. Even while the recipe of co-sponsorship and basic ingredients of academic work are generic constants, what and who is on hand at particular times and places substantially influence the kind of work that can get done.

Consider, for example, two of our case schools, Western Flagship and Eastern Elite.[8] Both are comprehensive research universities that have successfully maintained Title VI funding for multiple centers over several decades. The sheer fact of this consistent funding is, for many field experts, *prima facie* evidence of the quality of regional studies on the two campuses. The websites of both schools proudly portray long legacies of supporting international and transnational scholarship across disciplinary boundaries. Yet Eastern Elite and Western Flagship have entered the present academic era with very different endowments and capacities, and the way in which they manage the study of world regions starkly contrast.

Western Flagship is a public university in a vibrant and growing economic region. Located on the Pacific side of the Rockies, it has a relatively short history even by American standards, with a founding date near the beginning of the twentieth century. It is not one of the top two or three universities in the nation or the world, but it scores admirably on most ranking schemes, and tenure-line appointments to departments in the social sciences and humanities at Western would earn bragging rights in most disciplines. Western has a modest financial endowment per student, and over the last decade, in response to steady decline in state legislature appropriations, the university has become substantially dependent on tuition as a primary revenue stream. But Western also enjoys high regard among philanthropies and foundations in its region and secures steady streams of grant money from federal research agencies.

The seed of Western Flagship's now extensive regional studies programming began in the early twentieth century with the founding of an "Oriental" institute for the study of the languages, history, and civilizations of what was then known as the Far East. This institute was the organizational vehicle for decades of substantial government and foundation funding that flowed to research universities to support regional inquiry during World War II and the Cold War. The geographical purview of the original institute grew incrementally over the decades to include central Asia, the Soviet Union, and the Middle East. The name of the unit was revised occasionally to acknowledge its expanding territorial reach as well as changes in intellectual fashion. The "Oriental" in the unit's name became "Asia" during World War II and "International" in the 1970s.

Soon thereafter, a consequential decision was made to organize the institute as a department, housed within the arts-and-sciences core of the university. All Title VI–funded regional studies centers are seated administratively within in this department. This managerial strategy is important because it enables the unit *to act* as a department even though it is not called one by name. It can lobby other constituencies within the university and appoint tenure-line faculty on its own or (more commonly) jointly with other tenure-granting units on campus. The ability to act collectively as a department gives the regional programs at Western Flagship a high degree of political influence that is distinctive among our case schools.

According to our interview respondents, this capacity has been very fateful for the unfolding history of regional studies at Western Flagship. The director of Western's Russia/Eurasia center spoke at length about efforts of his department to work collectively and proactively:

> We have had quite a lot [of hires] of late but it's happened because of the—it's happened because of counter offers and what's taken place now in three different contexts. I can just tell you, Korean studies, South Asian studies, and our own program, is that the directors or key individuals in the programs had either contacts with the community that were considered incredibly valuable to the university or outside offers from another place or both, and

what that did was put enormous pressure on the administration of [the school of] arts and sciences to do something about these programs that were still surviving in all three cases on personnel who had been around for many decades. In the case of South Asia actually—the key people had already left, had retired and so for a couple of years [and then our new department chair] came and basically saved the program, [he is a] really well known South Asia historian, and a few other good people. . . . Essentially Korean studies was down to a single individual in the [department]. And our own program we had a number of people leave . . . so we all basically got out there entrepreneurially and . . . we just fought like crazy. I mean, I think, it's fair to say, so it's not exactly a secret. It's all public knowledge. We went to the community, all three of us went to the communities that were interested in the region, did a lot a ground-up politics making sure there were constituencies that were mobilized for these programs, going out and spreading the word to any part of the administration here that would listen that if you really destroyed this incredible tradition of Western Flagship in all three areas you would miss something. I mean, especially in the 21st century, with globalization as the buzzword and correctly so, you know, that it would just be insane for us to destroy in effect our accumulated library resources with no scholars to use them, our Title VI centers, which were world renowned etc., etc. So now we are hiring quite a lot in [the department] and have been really for the last three or four years. There has been a spate of hires to the point where other social science departments are quite upset. They feel [our department] now gets all the resources. So the issue has sort of turned around to the one that, you will never get this at any other university, but it's the political scientists and sociologists saying, "Why are all these people getting hired in area studies? Why don't we ever get a hire?"

This director was clearly pleased at his colleagues' ability to cooperate for appointments and maintain the vitality of regional programs. While we do not doubt their strategic acumen, our emphasis here is that Western Flagship assembled regional inquiry into a form that gives it distinctive capacities for cooperation and competition.

This same director went on to explain how he personally had used that department form to bargain and barter with other units:

So how I've handled that personally, I can't speak for . . . the folks in South Asia or Korea as much, but how we are dealing with that in our program is I have tried to spread the wealth that we now have, so that everyone wins, because my whole view of these centers and of area studies always has been that it's positive sum and anyone who thought there was some kind of bizarre civil war between area studies and the disciplines didn't know what they were talking about. If you hire the right people, everyone gets to see both a region in depth and some theoretical issues that emerge naturally from studying that region. So we have hired, I mean, our four hires which have been pledged, three of which are now about to be finished, the first was [name]. . . . And he is just unbelievable, I couldn't be happier. Really if I had to pick or design you know a person to hire in History. . . . Here is a person who is not only fluent in Arabic and Persian [but also] Uzbek, Russian, and German, and English . . .

INTERVIEWER: So these hires are directly through [the international department]?

INTERVIEWEE: Well not quite. I am sorry, I didn't mean to go into all the details of the hires but the administrative point you are asking is somehow connected to this issue. So what I meant to say was the first hire is a History hire, [this guy] is 100 percent in History, but he also does Middle East stuff and we got him added essentially to a search for Middle East politics. They hired two instead of one, and the reason was I could make the case he would fill a huge gap in Central Asian studies and trans-boundary issues, that is a person who could speak to both Middle East and South Asia and Central Asia.

Note that this director describes the hires as joint ventures. The history appointment is both "ours" and "100 percent in History." The capacity to work in this way with (other) departments makes for a distinctive variety of stone soup for regional studies programs at Western Flagship.

As was common at the public research institutions we studied, whose centers tended to have modest or nonexistent financial endowments, canny administrators at Western Flagship tried to leverage Title VI funds to attract faculty to the cause whenever they could. As Western's senior international officer explained:

One of the ways we internationalize the campus is direct a lot of the Title VI monies towards faculty who have hitherto not been involved. . . . And by throwing small pots of moneys at them we encourage them to teach classes for us that fit in with our mission. And increasingly that has meant we have reached out beyond the social sciences, arts and humanities to many of the professional schools for instance. So, we have extensive ties with the law school, we are very much involved with the school of public affairs. We have even made inroads into social work, education, nursing, public health. And so that's another example of how we have really been at the center of internationalizing the campus.

Eastern Elite is a different concoction. One of the wealthiest academic institutions in the world with a history as old as the nation's, Eastern is an extraordinarily complicated university with myriad pockets of regional expertise and organizational capacity. Eastern first came to be regarded as a major center of learning during the civilizational era of US higher education, and to this day its denizens are justly proud of vast library, archival, and museum collections covering the entire Asian subcontinent. Federal investment in regional inquiry during the Cold War brought additional intellectual wealth, as Eastern positioned itself as a major source of expertise for virtually every international agency in Washington. More recent decades have brought a substantial influx of foundation and philanthropic gifts to Eastern and a growing proportion of donors from outside the United States. This richly layered legacy of investment makes Eastern a city of semi-independent academic houses, many of which are funded by substantial endowments of their own.

The directors of Eastern's Title VI–funded centers understand the wealth of assets available to their associated scholars, and see themselves as conduits for conveying those assets. "We have incredible resources at our disposal," said the associate director of Eastern's Middle East center:

When we have questions that we need answers to, we have people to go to who can answer them on every level. If we have a student who has had a schizophrenic break, there is a team of people that we can go to . . . we have deans of every variety who help us figure out complicated issues. So, as much as we may not have a lot of people on our staff, we are suspended in a very rich web of resources and I'm very aware of that.

Later, in a discussion of how the center makes use of the university library, she further emphasized her center's linking functions:

"[The librarians] have incredible resources and part of our budget goes to the Arabic division so it's just a question of making those linkages. . . . That's another example where we have these amazing resources and it's just a question of ensuring that there is adequate interface or whatever the appropriate word is, connection, linkages established.

In this rich environment, perks unimaginable at other universities come as a matter of course. "We asked our faculty member on our steering committee who is at the graduate school of design, could he recommend a graduate student to help design our posters for all of our events and seminars," this associate director explained. Her center subsequently hired a student from the region "who is helping us incorporate some kind of Middle East design elements into our PR stuff. That's a way of mobilizing . . . resources which are certainly there without making big staff investments."

Eastern Elite is a place where center directors have the luxury of complementing an already robust intellectual landscape. As the director of Eastern's Latin America center said:

> We also have to spend a great deal of time identifying . . . gaps in the curriculum, places where there's interesting research being done, but it's not represented on the [university] faculty, and we try to deploy resources in order to make it possible to hire senior faculty in those areas.

This director understood that his was a special kind of job. "I don't claim any special virtue," he said later in an extended discussion of his ambitions for the center. "I think people who feel this way at other universities are trapped by a lack of resources. If you have a $4 million annual budget you can have a much bigger tent than somebody who's got a $200,000 budget."

Eastern's wealth has consequences for its stone-soup routines. Abundant resources can be a disincentive to cooperate with other units, as the faculty director of Eastern's Russia/Eurasia center explained:

> In the 90s, as universities got richer, certainly [this university] got much richer, it meant that there was more money available to do almost everything. . . . We sometimes do like a speaker's series together but sometimes you feel like it's almost not worth the coordination cost. If you want to do it you can kind of just do it. We made a big effort with Central Asia with the Center for Middle East Studies. About ten years ago, we established a little program and we both threw a few thousand dollars into the pot, but in the end we ended up doing virtually all of it ourselves. . . . They have their hands full with the Arab Middle East, and, you know, Iran, and so rather than worry about it, we just basically supported ourselves.

The financial endowments that make much of academic life easier at Eastern also come with their own integuments, as the associate director of Eastern's Middle East center pointed out:

We can't just go willy-nilly out running around with a tin can asking for money. Every gift that comes in [to this university] has to be . . . channeled and vetted by our development office. . . . We have very, very specific constraints about how we can do fundraising using our alumni. . . . We are not free agents in terms of our funding. You should underline that.

Yet even at Eastern, centers' reliance on the participation of tenure-line faculty for legitimacy and prestige obliges them to work in concert with academic departments. This same associate director made the point very clearly when she disputed the terms of one of our standard interview questions.

INTERVIEWER: Do you see these relationships with the different departments—with the academic departments—as enhancing or detracting from the teaching and production of knowledge on the Middle East on this campus?

ASSOCIATE DIRECTOR: I don't know who wrote that question. . . . Because we couldn't exist without those relationships.

INTERVIEWER: Well good, that's good, that's enhancing then.

ASSOCIATE DIRECTOR: Well, enhancing is too weak a word. It constitutes, I would say.

INTERVIEWER: Great. Then the other question to this, which actually I'm laughing, but I'm going to test it out on you. What impact does it have on promoting Middle East studies on your campus? But I think it's exactly what you said, it's necessary to promote . . .

ASSOCIATE DIRECTOR: Well, that's an interesting question because I actually think that may work to diffuse our interest rather than to concentrate it because departments have a lot of power. Right?

INTERVIEWER: Right.

ASSOCIATE DIRECTOR: But centers have to garner, have to kind of mobilize their resources to have power. We are only as strong as the senior faculty who are affiliated with the center, right? And the senior faculty all have departmental homes. So we depend on the investment and encouragement of senior faculty, but, you know, to be perfectly frank, if the senior faculty decided to mobilize on behalf of something else, we would be sunk. So we could use some more, in my opinion, some more kind of institutional force, power, connection because we are this kind of satellite. We are not like a department, you know, we are not a department. And so that's, you know, centers can be abolished, I mean, I guess departments can be abolished too, but if the center was abolished all of the senior faculty would still have jobs. Right? And they'd still have teaching loads, and they'd still have committees that they're on, and they'd still have students.

Regardless of the range and scale of resources available to Eastern's centers, the fact that they are not departments obliges them to participate in stone-soup exchanges with departmental faculty.

As even this brief comparison between Western Flagship and Eastern Elite suggests, resource variation influences the local character of stone soup, but not in a direct or linear way. The director of a Middle East center at a different private university, when speaking about a related research institute funded by an external donor, explained that the institute

> . . . has extraordinarily generous funding from outside. But it is completely independent of the university as far as I can see. Might as well be on Mars, for its connection to the university. We can't benefit from them. They don't connect with us. . . . They are out in another world.

In the joint interview a colleague chimed in, "They don't share any funding, they don't share anything." The luxury of more elaborate organizational structures can inhibit collaboration, creating more boundaries to cross.

Individual personalities can matter a great deal as well. Who on a particular campus is willing, able, and interested in working on particular topics shapes the course of academic development. A Middle East director at a different public university, expressing frustration about how dependent centers are on "either Title VI, or the university's charity, the university's goodwill, or some of the departments," added:

> Also personalities are extremely important. Some of the deans are very international and some of the deans are not. Some of the chairs of the departments are very much in their own disciplines. They do not like multidisciplinarity, interdisciplinarity . . . so there has to be university offices which are really promoting interdisciplinary, multicultural, global . . .

An associate director of a Middle East center at a different public institution, when asked to talk about specific challenges in her relationships with departments, said bluntly, "I'd say the only problem is faculty personalities:

> There's nothing we can do [about those]. You can shoot them with niceness darts or something. I don't know what you could do, but

there's personality problems. Interpersonal problems, occasionally even political problems. We have one very nice faculty member who won't set foot in our center because he wrongly thinks that we are somehow linked to Arab governments, and he is a dissident in an Arab country and he doesn't want to associate with us. Perfectly nice person, and obviously misunderstands how our program works, but, the tenure system is what it is and you get some kind of strange people and there are some difficult personalities. I think this is probably true on every campus, but we have some really difficult people, so that is an impediment.

Directors and associate directors elsewhere cited the relative freedom from interpersonal conflicts as true assets of their campuses. The Middle East center director at a school we call Southern State volunteered:

> Another thing that's unique about us is we really just seem to get along with everybody else on campus, we don't have any drama. It's a politically boring place, but academically and administratively exciting. We have good working relationships with everybody. Some [universities] there are divisions between one department and another. Sometimes there's political divisions like over Arab–Israeli politics or things like that. We don't have any of that here. And everybody gets along, we work well together, and as a result of this also we have a lot of cross-regional, ethnic, disciplinary kinds of work. So we have a lot of people who do Arabic and Hebrew, or people who do Islamic and Jewish studies. We do a lot of this comparative stuff, which a lot of people can't do because they're kind of divided along, either administratively or politically or whatever.

Regardless of campus context, diplomatic directors identify and leverage intellectual affinities and faultlines among local personnel. Consider the thoughtfulness of this faculty director of a Russia/Eurasia center at yet another public university:

> Instead of thinking about area studies versus non-area studies. . . .
> Instead of thinking in categorical data terms, think in continuous-variable terms. Who has more contextual expertise? Who has less contextual expertise? The centers that wind up becoming vital are attentive to what that core competency is, but don't exclude, and rather include on the basis of the character of the problem that they need to study, that they need to engage, that they need to understand. . . . And it enables the construction of alliances where you wouldn't otherwise see it. For example, I mean the school of

social work here, you know, is quite American-focused. So one would think that it has nothing in common with area studies. But in fact there's an underlying epistemological similarity and that is, you need to understand problems in their place and in their context. And so by using the term contextual expertise we actually broaden the range of possible allies where area studies at one time would you know, lead some people to say, 'Uh, isn't that a quaint Orientalist notion?'

This director evidently understands the different languages through which academic colleagues might variably make sense of area studies (categorical vs. continuous variation, contextual expertise, Orientalism) and indicates ability to communicate with different potential partners in various ways. We can only speculate that such diplomacy is rewarded.

Not-Departments, Interdisciplinarity, and the Dual Academy

A central task of this book has been to reveal the organizational machinery for doing academic work that exists alongside academic departments. That machinery is extensive. The not-department form is an administrative staple of US higher education, as is the intramural co-sponsorship we described above. It is hard to imagine work in the contemporary university without these organizational technologies.

There has been much discussion in recent years about the relative virtues of disciplinary versus interdisciplinary inquiry—but far less investigation of how academic work is carried out on a day-to-day basis in the social sciences and humanities. Is there much difference, on the ground, between how discipline-identified academics and interdisciplinary ones go about the work of learning and writing and teaching? While it was not designed to address this question directly, we believe that our inquiry offers some telling insights on the matter.

Disciplinary and interdisciplinary organizational forms are not mutually exclusive. US research universities provide rich support for both of them simultaneously. The department structure firmly supports and rewards disciplinary inquiry by privileging scholarship produced for disciplinary audiences. The department remains the pinnacle of organizational recognition for domains of knowledge, and the virtual cartels departments have over tenure-line appointments both solidify and reproduce domain prestige. Discipline-based labor markets systematically encourage today's faculty to train graduate students toward eligibility for appointments in disciplinary departments. As we began to explain in Chapter 3 and will return to in Chapter 5, this has deep consequences for the ongoing evolution of academic knowledge.

Yet much as Jerry Jacobs suggested before us, surrounding disciplinary departments are swarms of not-departments: the centers, institutes, projects, and initiatives that give any great university much of its vitality and which, unconstrained by the status and evaluation regimes of disciplines, house and convey a wide range of interdisciplinary activity. It is important to keep in mind that faculty and students participate in disciplinary departments and interdisciplinary not-departments simultaneously. The entire enterprise is predicated on this simultaneity. From an organizational standpoint, disciplinary and interdisciplinary academic activities are two sides of the same coin.

Entrepreneurial academic players recognize this dual structure and use it to leverage their own intellectual and professional ambitions. Co-sponsorship is the adhesive that holds the duality together, as one senior international officer at a private university stated clearly to us. She said that interdisciplinarity is "the norm for research here" and that "initiatives are always jointly sponsored and jointly developed anyway. So the boundaries between academic disciplines and departments and area studies centers are fairly permeable in any case." As with so many others we listened to, she noted the decentralized character of her university administration. Co-sponsorship, she said, worked well in light of that decentralization:

> So every event, every workshop or conference—there was a big globalization project a couple of years ago—they are always sponsored by you know, six to ten different entities across campus. To do anything requires cobbling together support, financial and moral, from different parts of campus.

This obligation to cooperate encouraged all parties to be less "inward looking," she said, complimenting one center in particular, which "tends to be quite well integrated into broader campus issues, and comparative sorts of things."

This way of making sense of academic work came up so commonly in our interviews that we began to see it as a generic feature of US university life. Consider the director of a Middle East studies center director who describes his unit as "bit of shared geography" and a "vector for sharing and communication." He continued:

> What . . . faculty do within the framework of our activities here is very much up to them, very much up to what's going on in their particular neck of the woods. . . . If you've got somebody in the politics department who is interested in, I don't know, media, and

public formations or something like that, then it's often because I know these people and because they know me, that we are able to have the conversation about who else is around, graduate students, other faculty around, other people in various other parts of the university, people in neighboring universities, part of the broader community around who might be interesting participants, interlocutors, people to get on board . . . that's one thing that we do is interact with the actually existing interdisciplinarity that we have . . . going on around us. It's just to try and use our limited capacities and agencies here within the center, just to nudge things in directions that would seem to be, that would seem to involve greater numbers of people to greater effect. So that's . . . an informal way that we've got of managing and playing some role in shaping the great diversity of things that we have got going on here.

Center directors and associate directors assume the dual and anarchic features of their universities and exploit them. One center director at Western Flagship confessed that the formal organizational structure of his institution should require a multilevel approval process for lines or campus-wide initiatives, but on the ground that was not how things worked:

Technically that means that someone like myself should go first to [the] Director of the school, who should go to the Dean of Social Sciences, who should go to the Dean of Arts and Sciences, who should go to the Provost, you know, for lines or big strategic initiatives that are campus wide. Now that would be a nightmare if it actually ran like that because no one could do anything and fortunately it doesn't run like that. It is chaos a little bit by design and it works all right, you know, once you master it, it works fine and I would even go so far to say that there are some serious advantages of this model over some of the other ones I've seen that are sort of more logical from a flow-chart point of view. So the advantage is that because we have so many centers and because . . . the centers are collaborating on these conferences across the boundaries . . . we are never constrained by the administrative structure, we just go straight to the source.

"We piece it together from the ground up," he continued. "And what that does is it builds in interdisciplinarity."

CHAPTER 5

Numbers and Languages

Academics have long mused and often worried about their own in-tellectual cacophony. Clark Kerr, a chief architect of the California Master Plan for Higher Education, famously remarked that faculty had little more in common with one another than shared grievances about parking. He suggested that the organizational complexity of modern universities succeeded at least in keeping different kinds of scholars side by side.[1] At the height of the Cold War, British novelist C. P. Snow cautioned that academics had self-segregated into "two cultures"—one scientific, the other humanistic—harboring recipro-cal incomprehension and mistrust.[2] The 1980s and '90s witnessed a swell of calls for collaborative inquiry across disciplinary divides that many view as inimical to revelatory or even relevant scholarly in-sight.[3] Interdisciplinarity is now one of the official goals of US higher education, joining a family of others—*usable knowledge, innovation, diversity*—that provosts and presidents rarely miss an opportunity to declare.

When American university leaders chose to organize curriculum and research into disciplinary departments at the end of the nineteenth century, they created a system for the reproduction of scholarship that has had deep influence on academic careers ever since. Departmental organization by discipline strongly biases inquiry toward disciplinary abstractions—toward *certain kinds* of knowledge defined in disciplin-ary terms. Academics came to presume that their official discourse was primarily and even properly among disciplinary specialists. Other audiences and conversations became secondary. Young re-cruits to each discipline were encouraged to direct their inquiries neither on higher orders of generality nor on particular problems as they presented in the world beyond the academy. Mentors told them that problems defined in disciplinary vernaculars were the ones most valued by journal editors and faculty hiring committees.[4]

This system is very good at maintaining cumulative traditions of inquiry over time, but at any given moment the disciplinary bias can inhibit other important things from getting done. University patrons often want to pay for scholarship in the service of real-world problems: cooling the planet, curing cancer, winning wars. This is why administrators do not just talk about interdisciplinarity but actively encourage and enable it. Funders and donors would rarely have it any other way.[5]

Not-departments have been powerful tools for enabling teaching and scholarship trained on substantive rather than disciplinary problems. They provide a great deal of flexibility to ambitious administrators and entrepreneurial faculty who seek resources from outside the university. Not-departments facilitate intellectual commerce between academic units, providing highly legitimate platforms for communication and collaboration across disciplinary and other kinds of divides. So far we have emphasized how the United States academy's dual structure of departments and not-departments enables cooperation. But its capacity to do so has limits.

As incarnated by Title VI funding, area studies centers have been paradigmatic instances of the not-department form. Title VI was intended specifically to put disciplinary expertise in the service of geographically focused scholarship that might inform international policy. Yet even while the centers courted humanists and social scientists alike and were ecumenical about method, they have been utilized much more by anthropologists, historians, and humanists than by economists, political scientists, and sociologists. One of the guiding questions of our inquiry was to learn more about the reluctance of scholars in the nomothetic social sciences to take up the study of the Middle East region specifically. Why, after years of systematic encouragement of research on the Middle East, had the US produced so little economics, political science, and sociology on this part of the world?[6]

To find out, we conducted interviews with academic chairs of these departments at our eight case universities. These people are, by definition, elites in their fields: tenured members and leaders of departments at some of the most respected research institutions in the world. We asked them to talk about how scholarship with a regional focus was perceived by colleagues in their disciplines, and whether or how regional inquiry by doctoral students was supported within their departments. Interviews with deans of international, global, and interdisciplinary programs filled out the picture of the climate for regionally focused social science on these campuses, as did our interviews with center directors (most of whom were also faculty members) and the associate directors who did the day-to-day administration of center activity. These conversations revealed a lot about the intellectual and occupational organization of North American social science.

Put briefly, we find that studying a social science phenomenon as it is expressed in any region other than the United States, in any way other than as a generic case, is regarded at best as a professional risk for economists, political scientists, and sociologists in disciplinary departments. Within some of these departments and particularly among economists, a commitment to regionally specific work is regarded as professional heresy. This bias is a function of three factors: (1) the primacy of theoretical and quantitative modes of inquiry in these disciplines; (2) the large investment of time and energy associated with learning a second language; and (3) the status hierarchy of the department system itself, which in the social sciences systematically encourages US-national or place-neutral scholarship as a bet hedge in the fierce competition for jobs in disciplinary departments.

These findings offer an important caveat to our claims in the previous chapters about the collaborative capacity of the US academic system, with its dual structure of departments and not-departments and stone-soup norms for intramural cooperation. At least in economics, political science, and sociology, the imperative to secure prestigious first jobs and tenure for top students leads mentors to discourage contextually specific inquiry.

These findings also contribute to sociologists' growing understanding of academic evaluation. Research in this domain has revealed just how starkly academics' assessment of good work varies by discipline. Disciplines shape the epistemological presumptions, stylistic predilections, and very identities of scholars as they evaluate each other's work.[7] Our own inquiry reveals an additional dimension of variation in how scholarly quality is assessed. In economics, political science, and sociology, what counts as good scholarship is closely linked with the status system of the US social science academy, in which the most prestigious jobs are tenure-line appointments in disciplinary departments. What counts as good work is bound up with what disciplinary faculty believe are good jobs.

In what follows we first describe the primacy that the social science disciplines give to abstract theoretical knowledge over particularistic knowledge, and show how this value hierarchy creates conditions in which social scientists are typically skeptical of regional inquiry. We then explain how the evidentiary and technical requirements of quantitative versus qualitative analysis reinforce the distinction social scientists make between theoretical and particularistic knowledge. These requirements also encourage faculty mentors to view training to competence in quantitative versus qualitative inquiry as a binary choice for all but highly exceptional students. Next we investigate how the imperatives of job placement for graduate students and ranking schemes for departments reciprocally discourage contextually specific scholarship in the social sciences. We conclude by further considering the organizational basis of academics' assessments of good work.

Theory before Place

A defining ambition of social scientists over the twentieth century was to demonstrate that their intellectual problems were as coherent and measurable as those in other scientific domains. This ambition has been only partially and contingently realized, but the social sciences did accomplish institutionalization as disciplines. This accomplishment required the cumulative development of abstract knowledge of purportedly universal character. The social sciences could be scientific only insofar as economic, political, and social phenomena could be imagined as general and patterned. To be a member of one of these disciplines meant being able to see the world through the lens of its particular theoretical frameworks.[8]

By fundamental contrast, regional expertise sees the world through the lens of place. This has been true since the earliest expressions of civilizational study in US universities. Regional specialists of the nineteenth and early twentieth centuries were students of specific others, and their scholarly identities and prestige were grounded in claims to authentic engagement with those others. One was an expert because one had spent time in a region and had studied its artifacts, read and spoke its languages, knew its traditions, and could discern its native distinctions between a twitch and a wink of the eye.[9] Area studies as they were incarnated during the Cold War inherited and extended this tradition by supporting language training and regional travel. Back home and up to the present, the rationale for assembling scholarship and teaching by area is that specific regions, languages, historical traditions, and social institutions cohere in peculiar ways that are fateful for academic understanding and informed government policy.

This organizational distinction—between centers focused on the study of regional specificity and departments focused on the study of abstractions—neatly parallels a chronic tension characterizing the production of knowledge on human social life since the inception of that enterprise. The tension is between the analytic primacy of specific configurations of cultural and social phenomena, on the one hand, and the analytic primacy of generic features of those phenomena on the other. Historians, anthropologists, and other humanistic scholars often commit to the primacy of specifics. Economists, sociologists, and political scientists often commit to the primacy of patterned variation. Attention to consistency across multiple specific instances of a presumably generic phenomenon characterizes the latter mode of inquiry.[10] Both ways of doing scholarship have their partisans, both have been elaborately critiqued,[11] and both have long coexisted on university campuses, perhaps always with the awkwardness we heard in our fieldwork. The associate director of a Middle East center, herself a tenured professor of Ottoman literature, was especially articulate in describing it:

> There seems to be this perception out there that centers do a good job of dealing with the humanities aspects, the cultures and languages and literatures and so forth, and seem to be less tied in to the social sciences. There are two answers to that in my mind, and one answer is that some of the social science disciplines have come to conceive of what they do so much in terms of an abstract set of methodologies that are unmoored from time and place that when they think about building their programs and what a contribution to knowledge is in their programs, they don't think of it in terms of knowing something new or different about, let's say, Iraq in 1940. If you're a political scientist, a contribution to knowledge is not understanding something new and different about Lebanon or Iraq. A contribution to knowledge is developing a new theory of democracy . . . you may use Iraq as some part of your evidentiary [base], but the point is not to know something about Iraq. The point is to know something about, to add something in methodological [or] abstract terms. It's a sort of a meta-knowledge, if I can put it that way. So, part of the problem is that the disciplines, the social science disciplines, imagine themselves and imagine what knowledge is and what contribution to knowledge is in a different way. And of course then faculty members have to imagine what it is that they are doing as researchers in those terms if they hope to be advanced.

We heard many other faculty and administrators talk about a tendency of the social sciences to separate inquiry from context. A director of Russia/Eurasia center at an elite private university, and himself a political scientist, described it as "the professionalization of the social science disciplines:

> The increased concern with general, theoretical knowledge, with systematic social science methodologies, the desire for generalizability of research findings has exacerbated the tension between

disciplinary hiring priorities and area studies needs. And as a result, there's been a secular decline in area studies faculty strength across all the social sciences at [this university] and probably everywhere else. This is most evident in economics where many places don't have any area studies scholars.

The Middle East center director at the same university, a senior member of the history department, complained about the "disciplinary move" in the social sciences "away from specific knowledge . . . there is a move away from the specific and towards the general, to what some mistakenly call theory, to what some blindly call science"—a move he thought "eminently regrettable."

Almost uniformly, our respondents thought that the primacy of abstract over particularistic knowledge was most pronounced in economics, where scholars strongly identify with a universal methodology that can be applied to any context or topic and where graduate students are trained to be topical, not area, experts. One senior international officer at a large public university, himself a sociologist, quipped that economics was "like physics. It doesn't matter where you go." "Economics is a perennial problem," said a Russia/Eurasia center director, "because economics as you probably know, the field has oriented itself much more to general theories . . . it has very little interest in the region." Center directors repeatedly referred to economics departments with words like "problematic" and "impossible." One South Asia center director thought that economists imagine themselves to be "beyond place." A Middle East center administrator stated flatly that "the best economists don't do areas."

Interviews with economists affirmed that their discipline gives priority to abstract rather than particularistic knowledge. The field is not about specific economies or places but rather, as one department chair said, about "the theory, the models, the tools." "Economists are not multidisciplinary by nature," he said elsewhere, relating a dispute between the gender studies program at his university and the economics department: "Their perception of what economics is versus *our* perception of what economics is it's like two different worlds." Another economics chair made clear that the most important features of a problem to economists were the general ones, not the specifics:

A lot of economics deals with issues that transcend borders, I mean demand curves slope down here and they slope down in China and they slope down everyplace there is a market. . . . Certainly for development and transition economics obviously it's very important to have good institutional knowledge and knowledge of the area because those have become important factors. I mean for instance if you were studying demographic trends it might be useful to know whether the country is homogeneous with respect to religion or heterogeneous with respect to religion as different religions have different teachings about, say, birth control, family planning methods, so obviously that would be very important. . . . On the other hand it can become quite an investment to gain that kind of knowledge and you might be seen as relatively narrow.

Economics department chairs were very clear that their explanatory models had primacy. The world provides cases to test the models. As one of them put it, "To understand what their census statistics mean, I don't need to speak their language. This is just wrong." She acknowledged that cultural knowledge may be helpful in some cases, referring to a project she did on consumption patterns in India:

And so one of the things you had to know to make any sense out of the data was that there were these festivals where people spent a lot of money. So if you looked at somebody's spending over the year, there would be these big spikes that were associated with these holidays when you go out and buy new clothes, or you go out and buy a lot of food, or traditionally there are lots of weddings held at that particular time of the year. So you sort of had to know to figure out the data, but you could learn that without spending your whole life in that country.

But to this concession to culture, the economist added a critical line: "I just feel like some of these [area studies] people are trying to erect barriers to entry, to make their knowledge more valuable." Perhaps more diplomatically, another chair conceded that "economics is not done . . . empirically in a cultural vacuum, but I wouldn't say that culture is our number one constraint."

The swagger that so often vexes economists' colleagues in other disciplines is also reflected in scholarly citation patterns. Articles published in economics journals cite far fewer papers from different fields than those journals serving other disciplines.[12] The conceptual frameworks and academic language of economics are now preponderant in public discourse invoking the social sciences.[13] Many influential national government policy positions are occupied by professional economists. Since there is little question that economics is currently at a point of discursive and political dominance, we were not surprised that our economist respondents, and their detractors, stood out in our interviews.[14]

Economists received the most ire from regional specialists, yet we found parallel sentiment about a tension between disciplinary and regional inquiry among political scientists and sociologists as well. One political science chair invoked the old "soak and poke" derision of area-studies researchers who value long investment in soaking up local cultures and poking around in the field or in archives:

> There used to be and there still remains a divide between sort of the real area studies soak-and-poke folks who say 'this place is unique and . . . there's no generalizable explanations for things, you know . . . these are *my* peasants and I studied them or they are *my* labor unions and I know about them' . . . and there is not much comparison that's really valuable because as soon as you start to compare you lose all the richness and details and interpretive analysis . . . versus those who take a more theoretical approach, those who take a more true comparative approach saying, 'yes of course everything is different in certain respects but there [are] things you can generalize on.'

One Middle East center director at a different university, himself a highly decorated musicologist, thought that political scientists might specialize in one specific region initially in order to develop their theoretical arguments, but that geographic specialization was "not a route to career advancement":

> You don't make a career being a Syria specialist. You make a career being a political scientist who maybe at one point in their life has been to Syria, but then definitely needs to go on to somewhere else to prove that it can be done, that these skills can be brought to bear somewhere else.

He went on to explain that to be "properly theoretical" one must use theoretical tools in multiple places, refining the theories based on each place one studies. This, he believed, "prohibits people thinking of careers in area studies terms."

> I think it prohibits the kind of real sort of lifelong commitments to people and places that actually I think is rather an important thing about area studies. I think losing that or making people feel kind of guilty or worried about that I think it is a bit of a pickle. I think that when people come up for tenure reviews I think people like to be able to see people who have done—the second project has to look different from the first project, and so again I think this is a way in which people who've done something in one part of the Arab world would be very much obliged to do their next

project in some other part of the Arab world, or someone who's done something that's very area studies will feel that the next book has to be something that is much more general and theoretical.

In light of these words from an area specialist, a straightforward statement from the chair of the political science department at the same university seemed especially resonant. When speaking about hiring preferences in his department he said, "We want people who are truly doing wonderful work, who have the area knowledge, but also who are political scientists."

While interviews with political science chairs left little doubt about that discipline's universalistic ambitions, a strong comparative tradition makes political scientists friendlier than economists to regional inquiry. The political science chair at a large public university seemed proud when he told us that "there is probably not a department in the university that's more internationally oriented than [this] department." He described his department as having "a large comparative field of about fifteen faculty and a lot of graduate students, most of whom need to go abroad at least for limited periods," and who often turned to area studies centers to fund such travel. "I'm sympathetic to area studies," he said,

> . . . to the claims of area studies of detailed knowledge of a particular region of the world. But the tension you're describing exists here as well because, the area studies paradigm has been under attack and we certainly have faculty who aspire to nomothetic theories that apply universally and consider area knowledge not a necessity or even a nuisance, because it gets in the way of their generalizing, but I would say our faculty on the whole is, those in comparative, are oriented toward a particular area. They are sympathetic to area studies.

As with their colleagues in political science, sociologists were somewhat equivocal about the place of regional specialists in their programs. A chair of one of the most highly ranked sociology departments in the country easily rattled off a dozen faculty who studied in world regions beyond North America—including both their full names and their research sites. But she added, "Probably across the country there is more work on the US than there is elsewhere so [my] department would look unusual." Two other sociology chairs told us that the risk of doing international work came from the decidedly American and (to a lesser extent) European focus of their discipline. One said, "If one of our students wants to study education in Vietnam for example . . . I don't know how they would become connected and I don't see a critical mass of people that are doing work in Thailand, Cambodia etc." He suggested that such work would be hard to fit into disciplinary discourse. "I think if one person went and did it and they came and made a presentation at the ASA [American Sociological Association] meetings in one of the sociology of education section sessions that it would be an eyesore." The second chair explained that comparative work in sociology is primarily between Europe and the USA, "the idea being that if you look at European societies they are more like US society."

This tension between disciplinary and regionally specific knowledge is hardly a novel discovery. Even while academic area studies were ascending to their height of visibility during the Cold War, many scholars in the social science disciplines regarded them with suspicion. As the historian David Engerman explains, while the government agencies that were area studies patrons "wanted detailed knowledge of the language, culture, society, and political system—not cutting-edge academic research," disciplinary scholars found area studies scholarship to be "unsystematic, insular, and impressionistic."[15] Noted Asia scholar R. A. Palat has argued that disciplinary researchers often believe "that their colleagues in area studies programs are not equipped to provide insights relevant for the nomothetic social sciences as they spend inordinate amounts of time in particularistic investigations which detract them from the study of 'theory.'"[16] Our interviews indicate that area studies scholars maintain a sense that disciplinary faculty view them as not quite on par. The musicologist and Middle East center director we quoted previously talked about "the slightly low regard I feel Middle Eastern studies is held in," and his sense that, among disciplinary faculty, "area studies people are somehow not to be taken absolutely seriously."

Some believed that the wariness with which disciplinary faculty regarded regional scholarship had to do with the rise of ranking schemes as measures of quality. Third parties such as *US News* now routinely assign ranks to social science departments, and there is little question that rankings direct the attention of faculty and academic administrators.[17] So it is unsurprising to us that some of those we spoke with invoked rankings when discussing how regional scholarship was valued on their campuses. One vice provost for global affairs at a public university suggested that ranking schemes were not calibrated to recognize the scholarship fostered by the area studies centers. She suggested that if a prominent ranking scheme put departments "among the best in the country at collaborating with area studies programs" it would make a big difference. The fact that political science departments build their reputations on their domestic work "pushes against hiring and expanding into thinking about international areas," she said. The director of a Russia/Eurasia center suggested that it would be difficult for the disciplinary departments to compete nationally if they did not follow intellectual currents in their disciplines: "They have to follow the larger [trends] . . . their rankings depend on it. And it might be counter to national interest, which I think it certainly is. But try to convince a political scientist that the priority should be different, forget it."

Tools of the Trade

Exacerbating the tension between disciplinary abstraction and regional specialization are substantial differences in the technical skills required to pursue them. Scholarship is an act of production and it has costly resource requirements. One of the most substantial costs is time—something scholars subvent themselves through relatively low per-hour compensation for research, particularly when they are graduate students. Another cost is the effort of training to competence in the theories and methods of a particular field. This is part of why graduate school takes so long and why the overall opportunity costs of pursuing a doctorate are so high.

The increasing authority of numbers in modern societies is reflected in the rising expectations for quantitative methods training in social science doctoral programs, and the primacy of quantitative analysis in the fields of economics, political science, and sociology. Quantitative data now commonly are presumed to be better, clearer, and more reliable representations of reality than any other form of evidence. The preponderance and ubiquity of quantitative data, coupled with dramatic advances in computational technology and the sheer maturation of quantitative methods, have steadily raised the baselines of mathematical skill required to produce capable quantitative scholarship in the social sciences. Doctoral students now spend years of study acquiring what their mentors regard as even basic statistical capacity, and they will worry for the rest of their careers about keeping up with quantitative methodological developments in their fields. [18]

Accumulating qualitative data and becoming proficient in its analysis are similarly costly. However, the resource requirements of qualitative research are different. We here define "qualitative" data as any sort of empirical evidence that is not inscribed numerically. In social science, qualitative data almost always are linguistic texts: archival documents, transcriptions of interviews or field observations, books, and articles. Developing the skills required to do qualitative research is especially costly when it entails learning new languages. Consider the time and effort expended to become capable of conversing in local dialects, or reading ancient texts. Merely collecting qualitative data is costly as well. Consider the time and attention required to assemble or peruse a substantial archive, or of conducting definitive ethnographic fieldwork. Such costs represent investment in the study of *specific* people and places.

By contrast, the costs of quantitative scholarship are investments in technologies of inquiry that at least purport to be universal. Expertise in a particular quantitative method, such as event-history or regression discontinuity analysis, is presumed to be applicable to many empirical contexts wherever the requisite numerical data are available. While scholars who study specific world regions invest in learning languages and dialects, quantitative scholars invest in learning statistics: the meta-language of North American social science. This great difference, between the particularism of language and the universalism of numbers, has profound consequences for the organization of social science scholarship, for priorities senior faculty bring to the training of doctoral students, and for the intellectual identities of social scientists themselves.[19]

Social science department chairs clearly understand both the limits of graduate students' time and the variable rewards their disciplines give to quantitative versus language skills. The vice chair of a leading department of political science explained this tension quite clearly:

> One dilemma I see is that as the technical requirements of the discipline go up then a student who wants to have both [linguistic and quantitative skills] is caught between trying to take fourth year Chinese and third year stats. In other words if what we think is a good quantitative background used to be two courses in quantitative methods and it's now four, that starts to rub up against the student who wants to take third and fourth and fifth year language. I mean it's not impossible but you know what I mean? There was always that tension and that's just getting, it gets worse as the discipline of political science gets teched up. . . . And there are Chinese politics professors saying, you know, 'three years of Chinese is not good enough,' and there are methodology professors saying, 'two years of statistics is not good enough.'

Another political science chair talked about the division in his field between:

> people who often times are affiliated with area studies centers who think the best approach to this kind of work is a deep immersion

in a particular place, mastery of the language, deep knowledge of the culture and the history and out of that comes a deep acquaintance with one case and an ability to say powerful things about the single case. And that's the older tradition . . . and then there is a somewhat newer tradition, a more modern tradition, that tends to do, rather than ethnographic or field research, tends to do statistical analyses of multiple cases.

This chair reported that the tension was evident in decisions about graduate training. "If we are going to teach a core course on comparative politics, what should be in that, what methods should be in that? . . . What should we expect students to be able to do?" The senior international officer at a large public university said:

The tensions between the area studies programs and political science have actually increased in recent years rather than decreased, and that they actually had much better relations probably ten years ago, but as the field has moved towards this quantitative emphasis I think they have perceived that . . . if there is an area studies interest on behalf of any of their faculty it is secondary to their quantitative expertise.

People with appointments in area studies programs concurred that necessary investments in language skills could be substantial, especially for languages phonetically distant from English. As an associate director of a Middle East Studies center put it:

You don't produce somebody who is fluent in Arabic in two years. It just doesn't happen. I mean you may have the occasional subgenius who is really good at languages and if that's all they do, they are really good in two years. But you are not going to create an army of those. . . . And you are not going to create a cadre of people that can just do the basic groundwork that the government needs right now . . . I mean that's a real problem. It's something we grapple with here all the time.

Perhaps not surprisingly, given their official charge of facilitating language instruction, center personnel complained about what they perceived to be the low status of language learning as an academic endeavor. The associate director of a Middle East center asserted that Americans have a tendency to think of language instruction as

. . . not really an intellectual activity but as a technical activity . . . [although] it's hard work and time consuming and involves a very particular skill set, [it] isn't a real intellectual activity like, oh I don't know, writing a history book is a real intellectual activity . . .

partly that represents changes in the point of view about what legitimate forms of intellectual activity are.

Investment in linguistic or statistical skill consistently was framed as a tradeoff by department chairs. An economics chair said,

> We couldn't really in good conscience encourage somebody to go out and do something like learn another language from scratch, because they wouldn't get any credit for it in the economics marketplace. They would get credit for the content of the research and not its focus on a particular area or language.

The chair of a top sociology department said that he discouraged US nationals from working on China:

> . . . because the Chinese sociologists can run circles around them unless they are really skilled in language acquisition and started early. . . . Or even undergraduates unless they're really, really dedicated. I do not advise they do it.

Whether they liked it or not, there was general agreement among our respondents that social-science departments prioritize quantitative skills over those required for pursuit of particularistic inquiry abroad. We here quote at length from a long-time senior international officer at a prestigious private university, someone who had devoted her own highly prominent academic career in international relations to the support of regional scholarship:

> You also have over the last thirty years just incredible opportunities in methodological terms with new computing power so the incentives have been very much to develop and push methods that are basically defined by numbers. Now you can manipulate huge datasets, so you want to have huge datasets and you want to play with huge datasets and so forth and so on. So it's kind of a push and pull, the push out of 'I don't want to have to deal with the policy people,' on the one hand, and the pull into the glamour and excitement and so forth the what-you-can-do with big datasets and computing power. . . . All of that has meant that the sort of messiness of the world outside the United States, and the datasets that are available about the world outside the United States, has just been demoralizing. If you want to be a hotshot political scientist you want something where you can cleanly describe hundreds of thousands of data points, whether they are votes in Congress, or surveys of opinion, or whatever they are, that's really fun . . . I can understand why that's fun. That really is leading edge, using new technologies. . . . But it also means that all of the incentives are

aligned away from trying to think about the Middle East, where there is not a data point. . . . Nobody does surveys or, you know, economics data is completely, it's not just dirty, it's filthy. I mean it's not worth looking at it.

The rewards that accrue to those using large, 'clean' datasets combined with the paucity of such data on many parts of the world to discourage regionally focused inquiry.

Good Jobs

All of this has consequences for the most fundamental academic process: reproduction. The transmission of identity, security, and prestige across generations has very high priority in most scholarly biographies. As individuals, senior faculty seek to continue their intellectual legacies into future generations. Collectively they seek to build the stature of their departments by placing students at prestigious schools. They pursue these goals by carefully grooming students in preparation for academic labor markets.

The top-tier occupational niche in academic social science is a tenured appointment in a disciplinary department. Tenured departmental faculty are the academy's Brahmin class, endowed with great autonomy over their own time, the specification of curriculum, the training of protégés, and the appointment of their own replacements. Of course, not all jobs in this niche are equal. The relative status of tenure-line jobs varies substantially by school type, admissions selectivity, institutional wealth, and academic reputation. In its variety but also in its steep hierarchy, US higher education is internationally distinctive. Essential to the task of mentoring is making sure that one's students are placed at the highest levels possible in this hierarchy. Additionally, on every campus, tenure-line faculty share the workplace with a large and growing number of people with other kinds of appointments: lecturerships, postdocs, and myriad research and administrative positions. These jobs grant academic berth and a good measure of scholarly legitimacy even while they uniformly have lower status than tenure-line appointments. This is the complicated, elaborately stratified world senior faculty are preparing their students to enter.

Chairs recognize that the reputations of their departments are directly implicated in student job placements. It is no accident that top departments are so incestuous about hiring junior faculty only from programs of similar prestige. Just as in markets for marital partners, where people consistently choose mates who are socioeconomically similar to themselves, parties in academic job markets understand that their own status is closely associated with how employment matches are made.[20] Ambitious departments make it their business to place top students in the most prestigious departments and universities possible. How disciplinary departments train their next generation of scholars—what Germans call the *Nachwuchs*, those who will grow into the field—reveals quite a lot about the status dynamics of the entire academic system.[21]

Social science department chairs made clear that they discourage students from focusing on international research because their disciplines' cores are organized around US domestic issues. This came up most explicitly in our interviews with sociology chairs. The sociology job market favors domestic work because, as one chair said flatly, "The national discipline is still so preoccupied with American society." Another chair described sociology as having "always been ethnocentric, focused on the United States, and so the amount that most people know about any foreign country in terms of sociology is minimal." When talking about graduate students looking for jobs, he said, "For sociologists, to be competitive on the job market you need to learn to write and speak the lingo of ordinary sociological research and so in some ways you don't want them to become too tied into area specific workshops and programs." A third believed that the more competitive candidates are the ones who are interested in broad, nonregional issues: "There's probably more jobs for a sociologist who's interested in gender issues [who] happens to be doing work in, you know, Tunisia or Mexico or whatever, than for someone who's an expert in Mexico or Tunisia." Yet another sociology chair noted that faculty who do international work face a burden in justifying their contributions and making their work visible and respected by disciplinary audiences:

> There's so much background work you have to do just to sort of set the stage that I think it's easy for people to say, 'Well, why are you studying that? Why don't you just study US society which is really what we are all interested in?' I say that tongue in cheek. . . . It's easier. It's knowable, right? And you know we have all these processes and theories that are predicated on, at least Western, if not the US society, in particular. So I think there is an extra hurdle there, a burden, but it's an intellectual one.

Political science chairs were not as adamant in their cautions about international work, but they concurred that contributions to theoretical knowledge were essential. The chair of a political science department noted a "growing awareness of the significance of [regional] knowledge compared to a few years ago. . . . I mean, you can teach democratization theory, but at a certain point you have to be able to make it relevant to what's going on in the world. . . ."

A Russia/Eurasia center director quoted earlier, also a faculty member in his university's political science department, was pleased that his departmental colleagues had moved forward with appointments to regional specialists, but he made clear that the candidates had strong disciplinary credentials. "The two people that we made tenure-level offers to, who were specialists in Russian politics, were both people who are fully loaded with social science qualifications, and are highly regarded as general comparativists as well as Russia specialists."

In economics, scholarship on general models rather than specific places is firmly prioritized. One economics chair said that his discipline did not train in area studies but rather was organized around methodology and broad topical domains. He said flatly that "it's very unusual for economists to speak a foreign language and it is not required as part of our training . . ." but added that because the language of instruction in economics around the world is English, learning a foreign language is not necessary. True to the disciplinary swagger of economics we noted earlier, this chair was pleased that his discipline's unity is part of what made economics

> . . . so strong and powerful. Most economists are operating with a very similar model and it's a very parsimonious way . . . of thinking about the world. . . . Economists are kind of imperialists so we are willing to work on almost any topic, but we tend to just descend on it rather than collaborate.

A similar sentiment was expressed by another economics chair in his account of some visitors to his university's Latin America center:

> They're not the types of economists that we really want to attract. They're folks with that policy aspect to it. So they are interesting to have around for seminar, but they're not people you build a department around, from our perspective and I would bet for the [policy school] . . . they are thinking 'those are the kind of economists we want.' Well, they're not the kind that *we* want.

These are the disciplinary milieus senior faculty are preparing their best students to enter, and they are careful to put them in the most advantageous positions to do so. Balancing high levels of language training, fieldwork preparation and travel, mastery of disciplinary theories and current debates, and methodological sophistication is a tall order. The chair of a leading political science department noted that "the challenges are formidable" for students who want to combine a regional specialization with disciplinary training:

> Particularly for graduate students who don't have the language firmly to start with, [they] have to learn the language. In the

discipline, they are also under a lot of pressure to learn different methodologies, particularly in formal methods and statistics and then . . . the learning of some of those languages takes a lot of time . . . [it] is almost like a zero-sum situation because the language acquisition takes so much time.

It means "mastery of two very complicated things. . . . It's a hard combination," a senior international officer said succinctly.

The conflict between needing to master disciplinary techniques while also building language skills and fieldwork time overseas is not limited to graduate students. Several chairs talked about comparable challenges for junior faculty, whose tenure clocks constrain the possibility of gaining new skills or conducting research travel. "It is always a challenge if you want to do a new language . . . particularly for junior faculty," explained the chair of an elite political science department. "It's very dangerous, given the tenure clock." The sociology chair at the same university emphatically stated that junior faculty could not expect to learn costly new skills before tenure:

> If they are going to work on those countries they need to come with the skills, they can't acquire them here. . . . You'd never get tenure if you were trying to learn Arabic. Hmm do I know any cases? I'm sure there are cases, but I can't think of any . . . it's clearly very rare. Oh no, no that's not quite true. I know someone. He's now [in another university]. [He] was working on colonialization across multiple, German colonies at multiple sites. One of them was China and he picked up a smattering of Chinese. [He] is an extremely exceptional person. He did that after he got tenure.

Several chairs suggested that at the tip-top of applicant pools were a few exceptional people who are able to master high-quality methodological and disciplinary training while also gaining deep contextual knowledge. But they are few and far between. When asked whether scholars might be able to combine regional specialization with core disciplinary training, this sociology chair conceded "it's a small elite that have been able to do that." His colleague, the political science chair, reflected similarly on this issue, "Most of us mortals are just that, mere mortals."

Academic Evaluation in a Disciplined Academy

Sociologists of knowledge have long understood that there is considerable variation across the academy in how good or even worthwhile scholarship is defined. While previous inquiries have analyzed variation of quality assessment primarily along disciplinary and methodological lines, our own inquiry reveals an additional line of difference in the terrain of academic evaluation—at least in the social sciences—between particularistic and universalistic modes of inquiry. This line is partly a legacy of the professional ambitions at the core of the social science disciplines to produce abstract knowledge, and partly a function of academic workplace organization that reinforces the primacy of disciplines over regions. Variation in how particularistic versus general disciplinary knowledge is assessed seems to parallel evaluators' positions in intramural labor arrangements that house abstract social science inquiry in disciplinary departments and regional inquiry outside of them.

The primacy of disciplinary over regional knowledge in the social sciences was so obvious to one Middle East center director, a historian with an endowed chair at an elite private university, that our questions about it elicited a wry response. He joked that economists were not just "difficult" but "impossible" to work with, relating back to our interviewer, "Have you ever had encounters with economists?" He then poked fun at our interviewer's efforts to probe more deeply into these dynamics:

> When you say, *"Really?"* it's like this is new to you. Please . . . don't pretend you are naïve [laughs]. I mean, there is a trend in political science to downplay the importance of area knowledge and . . . to emphasize quantitative things, which given the fact that nine tenths of the world doesn't have the data that would be required for their quantitative [analysis] basically restricts them to the United States and a couple of other advanced countries. . . . There are people who struggle with that within political science. Economics is a block.

He suggested that the best way to motivate the disciplines to engage with area studies was to offer money, to "dangle lollipops in front of their snubby noses. I mean, I can't think of any other way to do it." As he saw it, the role of area studies centers was to serve as a reminder that "the important thing is that there be deep knowledge, that there be language knowledge" and to help bring together "people who by the stupid narrowness of their disciplines don't tend to meet otherwise. We think those things are important, and that's what we do." That this respondent and so many others spoke of these matters with such vividness should not be surprising. Identity and emotion are intertwined fuels in the production of scholarship and its ongoing defense against criticism.[22]

What counts as good and worthwhile social science depends on where in the academic labor system one resides. On the topic of getting jobs, our department chairs were biased sources. Their leadership positions in top social science departments predisposed them to make disciplinary priorities their own. Other interviewees pointed out that area-oriented social scientists had jobs in the academy even if they were unlikely to be housed in disciplinary departments. Instead they might have appointments in professional schools of public policy or education, or in the not-department units devoted to regional inquiry. As one South Asian studies center director said:

> I am an economist by training . . . but I would never fit in an economics department. So in a sense we have moved it out of economics departments to be focused on the kinds of issues that we want to be talking about. . . . A number of us do development and a number of us actually do fairly careful economic work but we don't fit in the discipline of economics.

One Russia/Eurasia center director at an elite private university said "There are economists who do transitional economies and so forth, it's just that they won't be applying to our economics department. They might be appointed say at the [name of policy] school."

Those social scientists who also were area center directors or associate directors used terms like "natural" and "allies" to refer to social scientists throughout the university who either did regionally focused work themselves or could appreciate it in others. The director of another center at this same university, a prominent economic historian, explained:

> The natural association is the one between people whose knowledge is culturally and linguistically specific, and the people in the professional schools who do applied research, but the structures of universities are such that Middle Eastern centers tend to get stuck in arts and sciences, and they have immense difficulties, bureaucratic and other, to link up with the people who actually use culturally specific information and knowledge in the research that they do. So they are stuck in faculties with people who tend to look at numbers and graphs, which are not culturally specific. So I think the challenge that area studies centers face is to create more creative links with people for whom culturally specific knowledge and language study is important for their research. So, you'd be hard pressed to find somebody in . . . the economics department that thinks of himself or herself, mostly himself, as a specialist in Latin America, but if you go to the [name of policy] school, there

are four economists who are policy and development economists who work mostly on Latin America. . . . Similarly if you go to the Sociology department, Sociology is a notoriously ethnocentric field, and they have very few area specialists. You'd find very few people that know anything about Latin America or any other region, but if you go to the education school you find education sociologists that work in Latin America. So, area studies centers have something that naturally links them to the professional schools.

Universities do find room for regionally oriented social scientists, if perhaps only occasionally within the economics, political science, and sociology departments at their arts-and-sciences cores. Instead they pursue a variety of strategies to create homes for more particularistic scholarship. Joint appointments are one strategy, as a center administrator for South Asian studies put it, of "deflecting the worst instincts of departments." Maintaining not-departments is another broad avenue. So too are appointments in professional schools.

This way of organizing regional inquiry evidently has consequences for the identities of scholars themselves. Consider this account of a scholarly exchange, given to us by a director of Middle East studies center who is himself a historian. "I think there is an identity issue," he said:

> I was talking to someone we—we were having lunch. And this is someone who—every article or book they have ever published is on one Middle Eastern country. And we were talking and—in a conversation, I said—I referred to the person as a specialist of this country. And his back kind of stiffened, and he is like 'no, I am not a Middle East specialist.' And I—every single thing you published is on the Middle East! But it's—it's an identity thing. It's—when you are—in those fields you are supposed to be a theorist. You are not supposed to be in a box that 'I do Middle East' or 'I do Latin America' or 'I do Mexico' or 'I do Germany.' You are supposed to be someone who can do it globally, right? And so I think the theory fields tend to be that way. And the social sciences all have that tendency.

It all goes together. The conceptual hierarchies within the disciplinary social sciences, in which theoretical abstractions and quantitative forms of knowledge are given priority over particularistic and linguistic forms, are reinforced by the organizational and prestige structure of universities and, in turn, by the status politics inherent in academic identities. All of it has consequences for how faculty assess scholarly quality and how they train the next generation.

CHAPTER 6

US Universities in the World

By the time we started studying them, the eight universities glimpsed in these pages had accumulated a great deal of capacity for making knowledge about the rest of the world. The early American academics who built out the civilizational schema had left enduring commitments to the historical and humanistic study of others, as well as substantial and occasionally exquisite collections of books, manuscripts, and other artifacts representing varied cultural legacies. Through the world wars and especially after World War II, architects of the national schema added programs for the social scientific study of world regions and federal patronage for linguistic and other instruction that might serve US interests abroad. Our specific focus has been the area studies centers funded by Title VI, but they are among many kinds of not-departments that mushroomed on university campuses during the 1960s and '70s. Modernization and development theories of many varieties, along with their traditions of critique, grew together in a highly revered and generously funded Cold War academy. The close of the Cold War and chronic contractions in state-government subsidy ended a golden era of academic prosperity, yet within a very few years US research institutions were substantially re-narrating their identities. Signaling a third schema of academic internationalism, institutional leaders began to make sense of themselves as "global" universities. They breathed fresh life into the university's medieval promise of cosmopolitanism by courting more foreign nationals to their campuses and sending ever more faculty and students abroad. They built strategic alliances with other national governments, opened satellite campuses in distant countries, and actively courted patrons from every corner of the world. And because these new international activities did not necessarily replace the prior ones, US universities grew ever more complex. They accumulated ever more ways of thinking about the world and more units for expanding their international reach.

In previous chapters we have revealed several important aspects of how universities make social knowledge about the world beyond US borders. We have shown that universities retain clear traces of very different schemata for representing the world as they move through time (Chapter 1), and that the Cold War decades were especially formative ones for the character of the universities American academics inhabit today (Chapter 2). We described how the intramural organizational ecologies of US universities are varied, complex, and productively competitive (Chapter 3). We detailed the cooperation norms that enable intramural units to work together routinely (Chapter 4). And we explained the several ways in which disciplinary departments of economics, political science, and sociology have remained ambivalent about regional inquiry outside the United States (Chapter 5). We conclude by considering how universities are responding to secular changes in the politics and patronage of the US academy, and suggest how social scientists, especially, might help to inform and direct the academic future.

After the Cold War

World War II repositioned the United States in global political geography. Far beyond consolidating and maintaining of the East/West boundary in Europe, the US government had some hand in virtually every facet of world affairs. Its official positions were sought, or imposed, on all manner of issues: agricultural development, cultural exchange, postcolonial transitions, global trade. As intellectual and political historians have elaborated in detail, the federal government relied heavily on universities to supply the human capital, technologies, and ideational frames necessary for twentieth-century US global supremacy. This was the period that gave rise to the organizational behemoth Clark Kerr called the multiversity, the institution that was many things to many parties but perhaps preponderantly the academic servant of Washington in a multifront, decades-long project of global governance. It was a heady time for US higher education, and the period in which area studies coalesced into the form we encountered as objects of study for this book.

The organizational expression of area studies within US universities was the outcome of a compact between multiple US government agencies, influential academics, and large philanthropies. The official goal was to produce knowledge that could inform US foreign policy and build social sciences as strategic tools in reserve for any future need. At the time of its negotiation, that compact seemed good for all parties. Government agencies would enjoy sophisticated insight to advance their causes in world affairs. Social scientists and their home institutions would accrete capacity and influence. Philanthropies would get credit for helping to build a virtuous progressive modernity.

The people whose words enliven our pages inherited these investments of the Cold War decades, in the form of organizational units devoted to regional inquiry. Yet by the time we began scheduling interviews in 2004, much had changed in the academic world around these people. Technological advances were transforming virtually all facets of economic activity, rewiring basic relationships between workers, employers, consumers, and places. Humanists and historians were digging ever more deeply into the imperial substrates of what had come to be called the postcolonial world, revealing ever more connections and interdependencies between geographically distant places. Spectacular new religious and military coalitions immune to national borders were reconfiguring international politics and upending any number of academic theories. All the while, human beings and their cultural artifacts were moving fluidly across virtually all distances and boundaries. For many, thinking about regions as coherent objects of study seemed properly to be a thing of the past.[1]

Conceived in this context, our own project was guided by two central inquiries. First, we wanted to know the fate of regionally focused scholarship in a new era of globalization. What was happening to the production of place-specific knowledge when so many features of social life were coming to be understood as geographically distributed and borderless? Second, we wanted to know why social scientists had been so equivocal about the study of world regions, particularly the Middle East and the larger Islamic world but also regional inquiry more generally. Below, in broad summary, is what we conclude.

New Patrons

The people we interviewed were working in an exceptionally dynamic higher education ecology. By the time we met them, the Cold War compact that had produced the modern US research university as we know it had substantially eroded. Levels of federal funding for research had not abated—but nor had they grown for decades, making competition for grants fiercer with each passing year. Public flagship universities were experiencing declines in funding from state legislatures. Rates of tuition at both public and private universities were steadily rising in excess of inflation. Seeking new forms of revenue to replace lost government subsidy and further burnish their own reputations, public flagship universities eagerly courted increasing proportions out-of-state student and—especially important for our purposes here—ever more students from overseas.

Faculty appointments, language-training programs, public-service initiatives, travel: all of these cost money. Area studies centers without substantial endowments of their own relied on government funds to support such activity. Since Title VI awards are allocated through a highly competitive process, center personnel were always thinking about ways to carry on without it. "I'm hopeful that even if we don't get the Title VI, the deans will continue with their commitment, so that the center can continue to function as a center, albeit at a reduced level," an Eastern Europe center director said. "You see, the center won't cease to exist, because it continues to exist; the question is, at what level will it exist." Directors knew that existence without funds would attenuate their carefully woven ties with faculty, students, and the world beyond their universities. As a Middle East center director at a large public university put it, "What makes the centers work is this common interest between the academics, and the government, and the public, and once the funding is eliminated, that common ground, a lot of it is just going to disappear." In the final years of our field work and for several years thereafter, federal funding for Title VI was cut substantially. This had direct implications for the centers we studied. "We are all shrinking nationwide," this center director said bluntly in a later interview, "The question is how to shrink." In doing so the centers bore witness to the very utility that makes not-departments valuable for academic planners. They can change in size and function in tandem with material circumstances. Compared with departments, whose tenured faculty and doctoral programs keep them hard-wired into general budgets, centers and their staff are fungible. This makes them highly vulnerable to shifts in government or philanthropic priority and easy targets for intramural reorganization schemes.

While they were recruiting more students from around the world and courting new donors for their programs back home, US universities also were expanding their physical presence abroad. Extending a long-standing American tradition of school-building as an act of entrepreneurship and regional development, ambitious universities were building satellite facilities—even whole new campuses—in Africa, the Persian Gulf, and East and Southeast Asia. Akin in many ways to the founding of new colleges on the US frontier, these off-shore endeavors are typically joint ventures, with regional and national governments finding their own utilities in the expansionist visions of charismatic academic leaders.[2] And of course the internet and its attendant digital technologies have created many more opportunities for US universities to reach international audiences. An explosion of interest and experimentation with massively open online courses (MOOCs) by elite research universities in 2012 proved short lived—but it nevertheless challenged the presumption that topnotch education necessarily requires physically co-present instructors and students in specific locations.[3] For centuries American academics burnished their prestige and cosmopolitanism by finding new ways to bring the world to their home campuses. But by the early 2000s an additional project had become *de rigueur*, indeed an obligation of institutional ambition: to distribute one's own university, and its brand, all over the world.

Some of our respondents believed that this activity was tied directly to the courtship of donors. One senior international officer at a Midwestern public flagship said bluntly that the international initiatives at his school were

> . . . something that I think the university can market. We have been asked increasingly to develop international programs for potential donors and for alums. . . . We get stuff all the time about "would you be interested in having a branch campus in the Emirates, in Singapore, in China, in Korea?"

China was evidently a particularly hungry partner. He continued:

> They want as much as we can do and we have done a lot . . . they want as much as we can give them. . . . We [hired] a person who has the title China coordinator and she is taking inventory of what we have on campus. It runs to sixty-five pages and sometimes it's a whole page for one project but sometimes its two or three projects to a page, so there's just an incredible amount.

His colleague, the director of the school's South Asia center, said "American universities have always responded to just what's in front of their face, and now it's China."

New Management

Five of the eight schools we studied had appointed a senior academic officer charged with "global" or "international" programming by the time we began our fieldwork, and their job, as one of them put it, was to "weave the place together":

> That's the only reason you need a provost . . . that's how I define my role. This office, the provost's office, has convening power and

if colleagues across campus are interested in a topic, or if we are interested in a topic centrally, we can convene people to get them going on things, and that's what we do.

The weave took take a different pattern than the one implied by academic centers named by geographic region. An international officer at a different university thought that "the way in which areas are being reconceptualized and creating new kinds of configurations is something that can be done only when there is some kind of intellectual leadership that's getting the centers together and thinking about, what kinds of new collaborations and associations do we need to propagate?" She believed that this was "an issue across the country, in how to organize international and area studies . . . I think it's a serious problem actually intellectually, not just structurally." She invoked the example of her university's work on national security threats as an organizing principle for new intramural collaborations:

> Really it's a kind of matchmaking or brokering of—particularly area studies and social science expertise on campus—and linking them up with modelers . . . who are doing various kinds of models relating to national security threats. So the modelers are very good computer people and they are themselves social scientists, but they are not really up on the latest social science theory and area studies information.

Almost everyone with whom we spoke noted shifting university priorities toward something called "global," however hazy that might be. The chair of the political science department at a public research university put it this way:

> There is a relatively new effort to really put [the university], both in sort of a PR sense but also in real concrete terms, as a leader in global, you know, being a global university, internationalizing [its] curriculum, focusing on international problems of substantial size and importance. So the institution has committed to really making a difference in global health. There are huge initiatives . . . with lots of money and coming from all directions.

The senior international officer at the same university referred to the institution's "global agenda" and called it a "large culture change project."

New ways of thinking about the world were influencing the organizational scaffolding supporting international scholarship in at least two ways. First, our respondents described a shift away from a clear focus on specific regions to initiatives emphasizing movements and flows across places. The chair of a sociology department described a move from regional projects toward what he called "interstitial areas" crossing national and regional boundaries. "We don't just think of the world in terms of 'well there is Latin America' and 'there is Eastern Europe' and so forth and so on. We have a lot of intellectual concerns that don't fit within any one of those boxes." Similar comments surfaced in interviews with administrators. "We want to do things that enable us to bring together two regions of the world that have always had a historic connection," explained the senior international officer elsewhere:

> There are strategic, geographical, political connections between and among regions that fly in the face of area studies definitions of what regions are . . . at the same time, this push towards thinking about regions in global terms as well as looking at the connections between and among regions and so we are not really working with static definitions of what areas are.

At another university, a former director of a South Asia center also anticipated a growing focus on cross-regional and comparative programming:

> I suspect that we are going to be looking at ever more cross-regional programming. . . . None of us that you are going to meet in this office are ever going to move away from an absolute commitment to area training in the sense of languages, and whatever in detail about our region, but our substantive issues are not confined within South Asian borders. . . . Our problems are not, our topics are not, South Asia specific. They are cross-regional, global.

Second, topical rather than regional themes were often invoked. Centers and degree programs organized around cross-national topics like the environment, terrorism, or simply "global studies" were common. As one senior international officer explained:

> The way that I am trying to articulate the vision for this university, if you listen to our president and provost for instance, they will say . . . the three areas in which we can make a difference in the world are in global health, environment, and information technologies. The piece that is important to me is that if we want to make a difference in the world in those areas, those areas of expertise have to be grounded in the foundation of knowledge that's generated by the area studies programs, the social sciences and the humanities, the knowledge about the world. So to my mind they are the platform upon which all the rest of this activity rests, if we are truly going to be effective in the world.

To some this change of emphasis seemed rapid, even rushed. The director of a Russia/Eurasia center talked about the emergence of a new major:

> We are moving at a rate I have never seen in my career here to institute a new degree program in Global Studies at [the university] . . . I've just never seen the amount of intense work, moving, you know, full steam ahead. The way they build a football stadium, that's the closest I have seen at [this university]. They will put up a stadium in about a year but I have never seen them do an academic program in a year. And that's what we are trying to do here.

Center personnel were well aware of these new ways of doing things. The associate director of a South Asia center talked about the recent creation of a new Vice Provost for Global Affairs at her university:

> The creation of that office institutionalizes something that was bouncing around the campus for years and . . . it took a little while for that to become kind of personified in this office, which is still defining itself, but I think the fact that the position exists . . . can be nothing but beneficial to the work that we do because it sort of provides a locus for that work.

That speaker was optimistic, but overall area studies personnel were equivocal about the new "global" offices and their accompanying narratives. While some saw fresh opportunity for people devoted to regional study, others expressed uncertainty about just how regional specialists would be written into new priorities. When, in a joint interview, we asked about how a Russia/Eurasia center fit within the larger set of international initiatives on campus the associate director responded curtly, *"Who the hell knows?"*

The director quickly chimed in with a different kind of response: "I was going to say it's not clear to us." The associate director later elaborated:

> The university's talked a lot about globalization and [an] international university, but I am not sure the university in its own mind really knows where they want to go or what they want to do. They have created new offices, the Vice President for International Relations, and moved all of the undergraduate international programs into an Office of Global Programs, study abroad, things like that. Very little contact with us other than, you know, 'Hi, I am here. I'm new. Let's have a little chat,' and that's been about

the extent of our interaction with them. . . . So I am not sure the university has thought about how we fit into what they view as the internationalization of the university.

Earlier in the interview, the associate director had conceded that his dean's priorities were "more thematic in a sense than region-ally structured," focused on issues such as economic and political development, human rights, and international security policy. Yet he believed he could still stress to students that regional knowledge remained critical to their academic lives:

You don't necessarily have to choose, you can do both . . . these are not mutually exclusive opportunities, career paths, paths of study. But I think very much that the school is moving towards a more practitioner-based, thematic, interdisciplinary way of teach-ing and away from what was before a much more regionally-based view of the world.

The director of a Latin America center at a large public university believed that there were different visions of how international studies should be organized at his institution, specifically about

. . . whether the role of regional area studies centers should remain healthy and strong as I think it should, or whether you should come up with thematic centers. It may be that institutionally it is easier to support one center on globalization than support two or four or five area studies centers . . .

Senior international officers understood that area studies programs could be worthy components of their new endeavors, but none of them said that the inherited form of centers defined by regions was ideal. Instead they offered cautious gestures toward change, like this one:

We are at a time now of a turning point for area studies programs, and that if . . . faculty in the area studies programs are capable of stepping up and saying 'we would like to be engaged across the in-stitution to provide this knowledge base for the rest of the institu-tional activities in engineering, in public policy, and medicine and so on' . . . then we could be seeing a really important sea change in American higher education. . . . If they fail to do that, I think they will disappear in significance, people will say 'well who the heck were they? They were the protectors and arbiters of certain kinds of disciplinary concepts and language arcaneness of some sort, and we don't need them anymore.' And I don't think it's going to be a long time before people say we don't need them anymore. The engineers will develop their own international expertise, their own context, and they will say . . . 'what can they tell me that I don't already know about China?' . . . It will require the area studies faculty being more proactive, more open, and more flexible about what they want to do.

At the time of their initial formation, area studies programs funded by Title VI were unqualified wins for their host universities. They came with the powerful scholarly rationales of modernization theory, the endorsement of top social scientists, and the imprimatur of government service. The programs endured and often flourished, contributing to graduate training, supporting academic travel, and nurturing intellectual vitality through myriad lectures, conferences, and coffee hours. They became enduring fixtures in the complex organizational ecosystems of their campuses, contributing to the depth, breadth, and sheer variety of academic niches that sustain academic endeavor.

Yet passing time has brought change in the environment of these ecosystems, raising hard questions for university planners about which components of academic life should be sustained as they are, which require makeovers or drastic rescues, and which will be allowed to die. Because they inhabit organizational units—not-departments—that are fungible by design, center personnel were the ones who most vividly expressed the anxiety that always accompanies environmental change.

Ambivalent Internationals in the Space of Opinion

From its beginning our inquiry has been concerned with social scientists' ambivalence about regional inquiry. Why, after years of incentive investment, have economists, political scientists, and sociologists produced so little research on regions important in their own right as well as strategically vital to US national security? Our answer is that the prestige of disciplinary departments is linked so closely with scholarly identities, institutional ranking schemes, and doctoral student job placements that attention to contextually specific problems rather than abstract disciplinary ones is a very hard sell to departmental faculty.

The accomplishment of disciplinary boundaries and institutional security for the social sciences has made it constitutionally more difficult to organize social knowledge along regional or topical lines. One political science chair summarized it for us:

I know that some universities have developed whole new schools in global studies and so forth. We're not doing that, but, there is a major effort, so I would say kind of trying to catch hold of and ride this current of enthusiasm for internationalization and globalization is a major issue. There is an enormous amount of lip service to interdisciplinarity, and some concrete efforts I think, but in my opinion the disciplines have got a stranglehold on it—and not necessarily a bad one either—but a stranglehold on the affections and attention of faculty. Universities can't really break through that because the disciplines train, promote, and reward the faculty members. Interdisciplinary groups don't do that, and in my own case, immigration is obviously an interdisciplinary sub-ject, and conferences I attend like the one this weekend has got so-ciologists, historians, geographers, economists, a whole range of people. So I'm inevitably involved in interdisciplinary work, but anything I've ever accomplished professionally is a result of the recognition I've gotten within the discipline. So, internationaliza-tion, globalization . . . what I see is a well-meaning, but largely futile effort to encourage interdisciplinary work.

However troubling this news may be for those who would like a more cosmopolitan social science, it comports both with prior theory on status dynamics in academic professions, and with the enduring marginality of regional inquiry in the North American academic world. As sociologist and regional specialist Charles Kurzman recently lamented, serious social science on Islam and the Middle East, for example, remains remarkably rare.[4] Our con-clusion is that the paucity of regionally oriented social science is not a failure of Title VI. It is instead a predictable outcome of an academic status system that privileges the study of disciplinary abstractions.

We would be remiss if we did not confess our own study's emphasis on scholarship taking place at the arts-and-sciences cores of the schools we studied. America's great research universities now sustain spectacularly complex knowledge ecologies, and disciplin-ary departments have no cartel on the production of social science. There are accomplished economists, sociologists, and political sci-entists in professional schools of business, education, information, law, medicine, and public policy. Although our project was not designed to assess it systematically, our interviewees volunteered numerous reports of professional schools being somewhat friend-lier to regionally focused social science. This too would comport with the general insight of knowledge production our inquiry has sustained. Explicitly charged with informing practice and training practitioners, professional schools do "applied" social science by definition. The sheer existence of professional schools better enables scholars with appointments in the arts-and-sciences core to indulge their preference for abstraction.

But is that the sort of social science we want?

Consider, for example, that the general failure of disciplinary social scientists to attend to Islam and the Middle East has probably made it easier for others to claim expertise on these topics. We conclude by suggesting the changing place of US research universities in the larger ecology of knowledge production. Sociologists Ronald Jacobs and Eleanor Townsley call it "the space of opinion"—the vast realm of public discourse where journalism, politics, and the academy intersect.[5] The space of opinion is where politicians, professional pundits, and laypeople go to obtain information and perspective on current affairs. This space has changed substantially in recent decades on two broad dimensions.

First, a whole new category of organizations—think tanks—have come to wield ever more influence over public discourse. Funded by private patrons and specifically intended to direct government policy and popular wisdom in line with specific ideological persuasions, think tanks now give respectable organizational footing to all manner of partisan experts.[6] Second, the scale and form of mainstream journalism have been transformed through digital media. The internet has made it possible for many versions of news to be conveyed through an essentially infinite number of vectors: print, television, and radio journalism is now conjoined with web venues and social media channels of ever expanding variety. Costs of entry into the space of opinion have been reduced nearly to zero. Wildly diverse versions of reality can now vie for global audiences with the minimal commitment of an e-mail account, a Facebook page, or a Twitter handle. In this new media ecosystem, no one or few sources of information can lay claim to truth or primacy.

This is the context in which Duke University sociologist Christopher Bail observed how anti-Muslim fringe organizations came to substantially influence what counted as truth about Islam in the years following the 9/11 attacks. As Bail explains in his aptly titled book, *Terrified*, spectacular events such as 9/11 are exploited by all media players as opportunities to incite the emotions of audiences. Feelings elicit attention. Prioritizing sensationalism over dispassionate critical dialogue, anti-Muslim fringe groups and mainstream media outlets cooperated to produce news that would rouse and rivet a shocked American public. Amplified over time through the innumerable channels of the digitized space of opinion, ideas that are heretical in academic circles–that Muslim religious (Shari'ah) law is antithetical to democracy, for example–achieved the status of popular wisdom and demonstrably influenced government policymaking.[7]

In retrospect it is impossible to know whether or how a more robust social science of the Islamic world might have influenced the evolution of national sentiment in the wake of 9/11. But we do know this: during the same years that the space of opinion underwent revolutionary change and expansion, catalyzing definitive change in how Americans made sense of the Arab world, academic economists, political scientists, and sociologists had very little expertise or professional incentive to contribute to the public discourse.

This observation raises another important question: what might the US federal government, or indeed any other patron, do to incentivize more regionally focused social science? The investigation just finished suggests a few insights. One option would be to seed the creation of academic departments specifically for substantive problems, whether in professional schools or at the arts-and-sciences core. This is the classic strategy for upgrading the status of an academic knowledge domain: provide it with a prestigious organizational unit and the means for its own intergenerational reproduction through doctoral training. Downsides of this strategy include the high costs of initial investment, maintenance, and failure. Departments peopled by tenured faculty and doctoral students are expensive, and embarrassing to close. They also inevitably participate in intramural status competitions for resources and prestige. It is not at all clear that having departments defined by substantive problems would upset an academic hierarchy organized fundamentally by abstractions, even if the particularist departments were given equal organizational footing. Faculty ensconced in the "purer" social science departments would likely consider those in particularist ones lesser neighbors and additional competitors for scarce resources. Those holding doctorates from particularist programs would be ideally suited only for jobs in other particularist units, which would be slim pickings absent a blanket commitment by a large portion of the research university population. Such have been the lessons of doctoral programs in race/ethnicity and gender/feminism.[8]

In theory one could go in the opposite direction, suspending any new investment in disciplinary departments and building an academy organized around topics, themes, and problems. For a few champions of interdisciplinarity this is not just a fanciful idea, but we have a hard time entertaining it. Disciplinary specialization is so deeply embedded in the scholarly identities, prestige systems, and reproduction machinery of the social sciences that it would be virtually impossible to undo by organizational fiat (even if this were to be deemed a good idea intellectually, a question on which we take no side). As we showed in earlier pages, the rise of third-party rankings of graduate programs in disciplinary departments has only abetted provosts' incentives to beef up those units. However paradoxically, the rankings so often bemoaned as crassly instrumental measures of academic value have encouraged university leaders to make deeper investments in disciplinary abstraction. Any tractable plan for directing social scientists toward substantive inquiry will have to work from the premise that disciplinary perpetuation through graduate departments is here to stay.

Just how many of these graduate departments the ecology of higher education in America can afford to sustain, however, has become a looming question. The extraordinary expansion of the social sciences during the Cold War was underwritten by massive investment in higher education by many branches of government and sustained through broadly distributed economic prosperity. Universities enjoyed great public admiration and trust. Their leaders were allowed to spend their budgets more or less as they chose, and they consistently chose to subsidize the status ambitions of tenured research faculty. Maintaining a doctoral program became a mark of status on its own: clear evidence that a department was participating in the production and reproduction of disciplinary knowledge.

The resource environment that long enabled the expansion of tenure lines in disciplinary departments no longer obtains. Yet professional academic status remains tied to tenured appointments in graduate departments and the placement of doctoral students in highly ranked disciplinary programs. Status is sticky. The academic prestige system has not evolved apace with the organizational ecology of US higher education—an ecology that affords ever fewer tenure-line research appointments in the arts-and-sciences core.[9]

We believe that this secular shift in the resource environment of US higher education provides fresh incentive for encouraging young social scientists to better investigate substantive problems in specific places all over the globe. A great inheritance of the twentieth century is that the rest of the world still admires our great universities. Everywhere, people dream of sending their children to our campuses. They want tastes of our academic banquet through online courses. They court our experts to consider their local affairs specifically, on site. Worldwide, governments are building new universities and growing existing ones, often hiring US consultants to help them approximate an American academic ideal. What will our most ambitious students have to offer these new patrons, in what languages, and on whose terms? Facing these questions squarely might transform parochial social sciences into truly global endeavors.

Methods and Data

The seventy-three interviews that comprise the original empirical evidence for this book were drawn from a larger project housed at the Social Science Research Council (SSRC) titled "The Production of Knowledge on World Regions." That project dates to a pilot inquiry on Middle East studies that began in 2000 with support from the Ford Foundation. Two grants from the US Department of Education funded data collection and analysis in two phases from 2004 to 2010—the period that includes collection of the interview data analyzed here. Subsequent funding from the Andrew W. Mellon Foundation in 2013–14 supported additional data analysis and project completion.

From its beginning our enterprise was purposed with mapping the evolution of interdisciplinarity and internationalization in US higher education, with a focus on the organization of the study of world regions. The focus on the Middle East and its contiguous regions on the Asian continent had two rationales. First, the collapse of the Soviet Union had raised deep questions in several academic fields about how to conceptualize Eastern Europe and the Middle East. Once strong national and political boundaries had become porous or nonexistent, new flows of people, capital, goods and services, and information were rewiring the institutional order of a vast geographic area. We hoped that our project could inform scholarly thinking about these phenomena as well as funding programs supporting inquiry about changing regions. Second, although the beginnings of this project predate it, 9/11 raised urgent national concerns about the breadth, depth, and quality of academic knowledge on Islam and the Middle East.

Research Design and Sampling

Cynthia Miller-Idriss designed the research reported here as a qualitative-comparative study of universities with multiple regional studies centers funded by Title VI. Schools were chosen to achieve a mix of public and private institutions, a mix of degree and non-degree granting programs and to maximize geographical distribution across the continental United States. Initial site selection took place in early 2005. During the first phase of data collection (Phase I, 2005–06) the team piloted a comparative design that aimed to situate Middle East centers within the intramural organizational ecology of each campus. SSRC staff researchers, all holding doctorates or pursuing graduate degrees, made one-week site visits to each campus. The visits included observation of center operations and scheduled activities, interviews with a range of faculty and staff involved in research or teaching about the Middle East, and interviews with vice provosts of international affairs, the directors of graduate study in social science departments, and (for comparison) leaders of Russia/Eurasia and Latin America centers. In total for Phase I we conducted thirty tape-recorded interviews, forty-seven interviews for which we recorded notes only, and focus groups with both graduate students and faculty affiliated with the Middle East Studies centers we visited.

On preliminary analysis of Phase I data, we decided to develop a comparison with geographically contiguous area studies centers. In subsequent site visits we dropped the Latin America centers and added South Asia centers. This second phase of data collection (Phase II, 2007) also received funding from the US Department of Education. During Phase II we widened the scope of the project beyond Middle East centers to focus on broader questions of interdisciplinarity and internationalization among the scholarly communities producing knowledge on world regions. We revisited four of the Phase I universities to collect additional data on centers representing contiguous world areas, and added two new universities at which centers dedicated to Middle East, Russia/Eurasia, and South Asia all were present. In total for Phase II we conducted forty-three tape-recorded interviews with sixty-one individuals, and forty-two interviews from which we made typewritten notes. We also conducted ten faculty focus groups and six student focus groups with eighty-two individuals with academic interests in any of the three target regions.

Figure A.1 describes the composition of the interview sample on which *Seeing the World* is based. These seventy-three interviews, with a total of eighty individuals, comprise

- *Title VI–funded center directors:* Usually tenured members of academic departments with subsidiary appointments as center directors
- *Title VI–funded center associate directors:* Full-time administrators who often hold a PhD in a specialization related to the region.

Table A.1: Interview Sample for *Seeing the World*

University	Area Studies Centers						Social Science Departments			Senior Administrators	
	Middle East		Russia/Eurasia		Latin America	South Asia	Political Science	Economics	Sociology		
Phase	I	II	I	II	I	II	II	II	II	I	II
U West	D, AD*, CA	AD*	D*	D*/AD	NA	D/AD	DC	DC	DC	Dn	ADn
Quadrangle	D*, AD, CA	D*/AD	D*	D*/AD/CA	D	D/AD	DC	DC	DC	D*	D*
Southern State	D*, CA*	D*/CA*	D*	D*/CA	NA	D/CA	DC	DC	DC	P	ADn/ADn
North Urban	D*, CA*	D*/CA*	D	D/CA, D	D	CA	DC	DC	DC	Dn*	Dn*
Open Plains	D, AD	\\	D	\\	D	\\	\\	\\	\\	VP	\\
Eastern Elite	D, AD	\\	D	\\	D	\\	\\	\\	\\	ADn	\\
Western Flagship	\\	NR	\\	D/AD	\\	D/AD	DC	DC	DC	\\	Dn, VP
Big State	\\	D/CA	\\	D/CA/CA	\\	D/FD	DC	DC	DC	\\	VP
Total	14	5	6	7	4	6	6	6	6	6	7	73

Notes: D: Director, AD: Associate Director, FD: Former Director, CA: Center Administrator, DC: Department Chair, Dn: Dean, ADn: Assistant or Associate Dean, P: Provost, VP: Vice Provost or Associate Provost.

We adopt generic versions of individuals' titles in an effort to maintain the anonymity of the campuses. Any center administrator who did not have the official title of Associate Director has been categorized as a Center Administrator.

A slash (/) indicates where a single interview was with multiple individuals.

A comma (,) is used to separate different interviews at the same time, or similar academic centers.

An asterisk (*) signals when the same individual was interviewed in both Phase I and II of the study.

Two backslashes (\\) indicate where an interview was not conducted because the campus was not visited during that phase of the study.

NR refers to interviews that were conducted informally but not recorded.

NA refers to instances where a center director declined to be interviewed for the study.

- *Chairs of academic departments* of economics, political science, and sociology.
- *Chief international officers (CIOs):* Appointments at or near provost level, typically with parallel tenured appointments in an academic department.

Interview Protocols, Data Cleaning, and Coding

Interview questions ranged from specific queries about the operational aspects of area studies centers to broader questions about challenges and issues related to internationalization on each campus and questions about the study of particular world regions on each campus. Interview protocols are included in the text that follows.

Data management and analysis was ongoing throughout the project. Interview and focus group data were transcribed and stored in password-protected digital folders on SSRC computer servers. We held a series of two-day, intensive "data camps" at the SSRC offices in New York, where the entire research team gathered to listen to transcripts, discuss coding and emerging themes, raise questions about data we needed to obtain, and brainstorm chapter and book outlines.

For the transcriptions of the seventy-three interviews used as evidence in this book, we worked with several doctoral-level research assistants to carefully check and clean transcriptions and develop an inductive coding scheme (using Atlas.ti) for systematic analysis. Interview transcripts were read multiple times by multiple team members to elicit patterns and key themes. Initial codes were always developed through multiple rounds of reading and team discussion. As a final check on accuracy, all quotations that appear in this book were compared against the original interview recordings.

Phase I Interview Instruments

INTERVIEW QUESTIONS

Director/Administrator

Explain SSRC evaluation. Review objectives: We are interested in knowing about the experiences of students and faculty who are studying the Middle East, as well as students who are from the region, at this university and about the role of your university in contributing to the study of the Middle

East and the Islamic world in general. Also, we are evaluating the Middle East Study Center in terms of two of the central purposes of area studies programs, achieving balance of interdisciplinary production of knowledge on the Middle East, and in terms of achieving the internationalization of the campus.

I. Center Structure, Mission, and Role

1a: Centers will be asked to provide a copy of their mission statement in advance of the interview. For those centers that have a mission statement: When was the mission statement formulated? Is it reflective of how you see/understand the role of the Center on campus? If not, how has the role of the Center changed since the creation of the mission statement? *If the Center does not have a mission statement: How do you describe the mission of your center? How do you understand the role of the Center on campus?*

1a-2: What is the scope of your center and is there a specific geographic focus (e.g., specific Middle East cultures, countries, subregions)? When and why was this focus chosen? Has the focus changed in any way over the past five years? If so, in what way(s)? and why?

1b: Please describe the structure and organization of your center. How does it relate to the central administration of the university and its schools, disciplinary departments, and other international studies centers?

1b-1: In your view, does your center's structure/organization have any significant effects on its functioning in various areas (e.g., institutional support, research agenda, faculty hiring and tenure decisions, representation of various disciplines, student enrollments)? If so, please describe any positive or negative effects as well as any plans for change. How does it have an impact on your mission?

1c: Are there adequate courses that focus on the Middle East to respond to student demand? Are there enough faculty in different disciplines who can advise student dissertations on the Middle East? To what extent do the various academic disciplines (especially economics, political science, and sociology) offer courses that focus on the Middle East? Are these kinds of courses crosslisted or co-taught (with your center)?

1d: What, if anything, has changed on campus since 9/11? For example, are there more speakers, more efforts to hire faculty with specialization in the Middle East, etc.? What has changed for your center since 9/11?

II. Center Autonomy and Interdisciplinarity

2a: Please describe your center's relationship with other academic departments on campus? For example, do you have any involvement in faculty hiring decisions? In the selection of students and the funding of students? In co-sponsoring guest speakers, visiting scholars, etc.? Do you have any influence over departments? Are any classes co-taught with faculty from other departments or are classes cross-listed with other departments? Dissertation committees?

2a-1: To what extent does this relationship vary by department? Which departments have stronger relationships with the Middle East Studies Center, and why? Does student use of the Center tend to be heavier from certain disciplines? If so, why do you think this is the case? (Do you see these relationships with academic departments as enhancing or detracting from the teaching and production of knowledge on the Middle East on this campus? What impact does that have on promoting Middle East studies on your campus?)

2a-2: Are there any special challenges or difficulties that arise from these relationships with departments (e.g., with regard to institutional support, faculty appointments and tenure decisions, curriculum and course development, research agenda, student enrollments and advising, etc.)?

2b: For degree granting programs: What kind of curricular control does the Center have over its own programs and over other degree program curricula? For example, does the Center have a role in selecting the courses that count for degree requirements?

2c: What is the Center's role vis-à-vis the university administration? How does the administration engage with the Center?

2d: How much autonomy does the Center have in terms of its finances, curriculum, or other decision making, such as student enrollment and funding? What do you see as the major constraints to this autonomy? What enables it?

2e: Does the Center receive funding aside from Title VI? What kinds of funding support the Center? Are there funds or resources that come directly from donors in the Middle East? How would you characterize the Center's relationship with donors?

III. The Center's Role vis-à-vis Other Units and Centers

The purpose is to map the landscape on these campuses—how well are they connected to other initiatives?

3a: Do you have a relationship with other area studies centers on campus? What about with other centers focused on subregional or national areas in the Middle East and thematic centers, such as religious study centers, conflict/peace study centers, or cross-boundary centers, such as migration or environmental study centers? Do area studies centers here get involved with these centers? Does your center?

3b: Does the Center engage with other university efforts to establish partnerships in the Middle East (e.g., satellite or branch campuses)?

3c: Have any new areas emerged on campus that focus on the Middle East or related areas? *Note for interviewer: Specifically in the last five years.* How did these come about? What has been the Center's role in facilitating the development of these programs?

3d: Are there any student-run forums or organizations that the Center sponsors? If so, what types of activities? Who is involved in these activities and do they involve students from other departments?

3e: Does the Center have any relationships with neighboring liberal arts colleges? If so, what is the nature of these relationships (sponsor events together, co-teach classes, etc.)?

IV. The Center's Role in Interfacing with International Initiatives

4a: What opportunities are available for faculty and students to travel to the Middle East for teaching, study, internships, practical training, and/or research? How does the Center facilitate these opportunities? Does the Center work with other university departments or study abroad programs to create more opportunities for students and faculty?

4b: *Redundant? Ask only if not answered in above section.* In the last five years, what role, if any, has the Center played in establishing or supporting collaborations with institutions in the Middle East (e.g., with regard to teaching, research, student and faculty exchanges, sharing of materials, conferences, and other significant activities)?

4b-1: Did the University recognize the significance of these collaborations? In what way? Please describe any difficulties that you may have had with these collaborations. Have the difficulties made you more or less reluctant to engage in future collaborations?

4c: Are there any other opportunities in or outside the region?

4d: How often does the Center host visiting faculty and sponsor visiting lectures? How have these initiatives been received by both students and faculty of the Center and the larger university? What type of effort has been made to recruit visiting scholars to the campus? How have these efforts been successful? How can these efforts be improved?

4e: Are there any other kinds of international visitors—foreign delegations of teachers, ambassadors, etc.?

V. Future Directions and Other Issues

5a: How typical is your center compared to other MES centers that you know? What is unique about your center?

5b: In your view, what are the main challenges confronting the field of Middle East studies in the next several years, both in general and on this campus and what can be done to meet these challenges?

5c: Do you have adequate staff support and student workers at your center? If not, what could be done to alleviate the problem or what could be reorganized? What does the Center need?

5d: Is there a lack of ME language teachers at this university? How does the lack of teachers affect students from other disciplines who may want to specialize in the Middle East Studies Center (e.g., there may not be enough classes, etc.)?

5e: Does the Center have any specific plans to establish new programs and services or to expand or improve existing ones?

5f: If you had more funding, what would you do? For example, in what ways would you expand the Center?

5g: Please make any additional comments you wish to about Middle East studies either in general or on this campus.

5h: Other questions specifically related to the Center.

5i: What sort of feedback from this evaluation would be helpful to you? Do you have any specific concerns/questions that should be included in our online survey?

Note to interviewer: Assess the extent to which area studies as a paradigm is challenged and questioned. With emphasis on Middle East studies, has 9/11 reaffirmed or weakened this paradigm?

Interview with Provost or International Administrator

Explain SSRC evaluation. Review objectives: We are interested in knowing about the experiences of students and faculty who are studying the Middle East, as well as students who are from the region, at this university and about the role of your university in contributing to the study of the Middle East and the Islamic world in general. Also, we are evaluating the Middle East Study Center in terms of two of the central purposes of area studies programs: achieving balance of interdisciplinary production of knowledge on the Middle East, and in terms of achieving internationalization of the campus.

Questions about International Initiatives and Middle East Studies on Campus: *First, I'd like to get your opinions about international initiatives and Middle East studies on campus more generally.*

1. ****Look for this information in the website and ask only if information is not publicly available****. What kinds of international initiatives are happening on campus around issues related to the Middle East, Islam, Arab Studies, etc. (e.g., partnerships with universities overseas, consulting on educational reform, cross-national exchanges, etc.)?

2. What have been the broad trends in international activities on this campus over the past five years? Are there new kinds of programs or new degrees that have been established that relate to international topics or to globalization, etc. (e.g., in Global Studies)? Where do area studies centers fit in with these trends? Has there been increased hiring for faculty in area studies and languages? For example, there is often a lack of language teachers; have more teachers been hired to respond to student demand?

3. What, if anything, has changed on campus since 9/11? What do you think has changed for teaching and research on the Middle East at this university? For example, are there more speakers, more efforts to hire faculty with specialization in the Middle East, etc.? Has there been an increased student demand for courses focused on the Middle East since 9/11? If so, how has the University responded to this demand?

4. One of the reasons we're interested in these questions is because currently there is an imbalance within the Middle East studies centers—that is, there are more students/graduates who focus on the humanities (religion, history, literature) and fewer who focus on the social sciences, specifically political science, sociology, and economics. Do you see anything specific in the [relevant Faculty or School] that contributes to this trend? In other words, are there structural or other deterrents to students' engagement with the region or with other international topics? Or specifically, are there any trends in the disciplines that hinder or prohibit an in-depth-focus of a Middle East region?

5. What can you tell me about your students from the Middle East region—in general, do they come from one specific region and background? How are they recruited and what sort of support and funding is available to them?

6. What can you tell me about the faculty from the region—are there initiatives to recruit faculty? *If they cannot comment about faculty from the region, ask for the name of the person who could address this question.*

Questions about the Center for Middle East Studies and Interdisciplinarity: *Now I'd like to ask you some questions that are more specifically related to the Center for Middle Eastern Studies (CMES) at this university.*

1. In general terms, how do you see the role of the CMES on campus?
2. How does your office work with CMES? What type of support do you provide?
3. How does CMES work with or collaborate with other centers? Does your office facilitate any of these collaborations?
4. Does your office facilitate any international initiatives with CMES?
5. In your view, what are the main challenges confronting area studies in the next several years, both in general and on this campus and what can be done to meet these challenges?

Please make any additional comments you wish about Middle East Studies or area studies either in general or on this campus.

Interviews with Directors of Russia/Eurasia and Latin America Centers

Explain SSRC evaluation. Review objectives: We are interested in knowing about the experiences of students who are studying the Middle East, as well as students who are from the region, at this university. Also, we are evaluating the Middle East study centers in terms of two of the central purposes of area studies programs: achieving balance of interdisciplinary production of knowledge on the Middle East, and in terms of achieving internationalization of the Center. By interviewing the directors of the Russia/Eurasia (and Latin America centers, we hope to gain a broader understanding of area studies in general on your campus.

I. Center Structure, Mission, and Role

1a: How would you describe the mission of your center? How do you understand the role of the Center on campus?

1b: Are there adequate courses that focus on the [*insert geographic region*] to respond to student demand? Are there enough faculty in different disciplines who can advise student dissertations on the [*region*]? To what extent do the various academic disciplines (especially economics, political science, and sociology) offer courses that focus on the [*region*]? Are these kinds of courses cross-listed or co-taught?

II. Center Autonomy and Interdisciplinarity

2a: Please describe your center's relationship with other academic departments on campus? For example, do you have any involvement in faculty hiring decisions? In the selection of students and the funding of students? In co-sponsoring guest speakers, visiting scholars, etc.? Do you have any influence over disciplinary over departments? Are there any cross-listed or co-taught courses?

2a-1: To what extent does this relationship vary by department? Which departments have stronger relationships with your center, and why? Does student use of the Center tend to be heavier from certain disciplines? If so, why do you think this is the case? Do you see these relationships with academic departments as enhancing or detracting from the teaching and production of knowledge on the [region] on this campus?

2b: What is the Center's role vis-à-vis the university administration? For example, is the Center involved in any way in helping set the agenda for the university in terms of international education, interdisciplinary linkages, or [region] studies? How does the administration engage with the Center?

2c: How much autonomy does the Center have in terms of its finances, curriculum, or other decision making, such as student enrollment and funding? What do you see as the major constraints to this autonomy? What enables it?

2d: Does the Center receive funding aside from Title VI? What kinds of funding support the Center? Are there funds or resources that come directly from donors in the [region]? How would you characterize the Center's relationship with donors?

III. The Center's Role vis-à-vis Other Units and Centers
The purpose is to map the landscape on these campuses—how well are they connected to other initiatives?

3a: Do you have a relationship with other area studies centers on campus? What about with other centers focused on subregional or national areas in the [region] and thematic centers, such as religious study centers, conflict/peace study centers, or cross-boundary centers, such as migration or environmental study centers?

IV. The Center's Role in Interfacing with International Initiatives
4a: What opportunities are available for faculty and students to travel to the [region] for teaching, study, internships, practical training and/or research? How does the Center facilitate these opportunities? Does the Center work with other university departments or study abroad programs to create more opportunities for students and faculty?

4b: How often does the Center host visiting faculty and sponsor visiting lectures? How have these initiatives been received by both students and faculty of the Center and the larger university? What type of effort has been made to recruit visiting scholars to the campus? How have these efforts been successful? How can these efforts be improved?

V. Future Directions and Other Issues

5a: How typical is your center compared to other centers that you know?

5b: In your view, what are the main challenges confronting area studies in the next several years, both in general and on this campus and what can be done to meet these challenges?

5c: One of the reasons why we're interested in these questions is because currently there is an imbalance within the Middle East studies centers—there are more students/graduates who focus on the humanities (religion, history, literature) and fewer who focus on the social sciences, specifically political science, sociology, and economics. Do you see anything specific in the [relevant Faculty or School] or in the disciplines that hinders or prohibits an in-depth-focus of the Middle East (or Latin America or former Soviet Union)?

5d: Please make any additional comments you wish about [region] studies either in general or on this campus.

Directors of Graduate Advising

Sociology, Economics, and Political Science Departments

Explain SSRC evaluation. Review objectives: We are interested in knowing about the experiences of students who are studying the Middle East, as well as students who are from the region, at this university. Also, we are evaluating the Middle East study centers in terms of two of the central purposes of area studies programs: achieving balance of interdisciplinary production of knowledge on the Middle East, and in terms of achieving the internationalization of the campus.

1. How many students do you have who are working on dissertations —or preparing for dissertation work—on a topic related to the Middle East? Has this number changed much over the past five years?

2. Do these students have trouble finding faculty with expertise in the region who can serve as advisors, dissertation committee members, etc.?

3. Do you find there is adequate support for students who want to do international fieldwork for their dissertations? For example, how easy is it for them to find funding to travel to the region for language training, research/fieldwork, conferences, etc.?

4. What kinds of challenges, if any, are involved with combining a regional specialization with disciplinary training in sociology/economics/political science? For example, is there adequate space in electives for language training?

5. Is there a requirement for foreign language proficiency or mastery for the degree?

6. What do you know about your graduate students' relationship with the Middle East Studies Center (meaning those students who are working on a topic related to the region)? Does the Center provide resources, faculty expertise, etc. to these students? What is still needed?

Individuals Who Organize Activities within CMES

These individuals may provide a richer understanding of how the Center is used and who uses the Center, and may help us map the Center on campus.

1. In general terms, what do you think is the Center's role at the University?

2. Outside of attending classes, please describe how students use the Center (e.g., lectures, fellowships, language training, hub for information, etc.)? How do faculty use the Center (e.g., for meetings, research), and what is the quality of these visits (are they substantive or just lunch)?

3. Specific question about the individual's project—e.g., what does the [relevant project] do? How and why was it started? Funding? Do you hire students to work for your (journal/research project/outreach work/etc.)? What departments do they typically come from?

4. Besides working for your [activity], do students from other departments participate in your [activity—journal, forums]? If so, how do they become involved and are they from any particular discipline?

5. In what ways do you work with other centers or departments?

6. What, if anything, has changed on campus since 9/11? For example, are there more speakers, more efforts to hire faculty with specialization in the Middle East, etc.? What has changed for your center since 9/11?

7. In your view, what are the main challenges confronting the field of Middle East studies in the next several years, both in general and on this campus and what can be done to meet these challenges?

8. Please make any additional comments you wish about Middle East studies either in general or on this campus.

9. What sort of feedback from this evaluation would be helpful to you? Do you have any specific concerns/questions that should be included in our online survey?

Landscape of Activities Related to the ME

These questions are aimed toward individuals who direct or organize projects related to the ME but are not part of CMES. Would these activities exist without CMES?

1. Specific question about the individual's department/project/ program/activity—e.g., please describe the actual activities in more detail. How and why was it started? Funding?
2. Do students from other departments participate in your department/ project/program/activity? If so, how do they become involved and are they from any particular discipline? Do you hire students to work for your department/project/program/activity? What departments do they typically come from?
3. As part of our evaluation of the CMES, we are trying to understand where knowledge about the Middle East is produced on campus and where teaching and learning about the ME takes places. Among the many activities related to the Middle East here on campus, is there a central hub for the production of this knowledge and for the training of students? What is this hub and what is its role on campus? *If the Center is the hub, ask:* How does the Center's role differ from the role of your department/project/program/ activity? *If the Center is not the hub, ask:* Please tell me about the Center's role in relation to this hub, and in general terms, what do you think is the Center's role at the University?
4. In what ways do you work with other centers or departments?
5. What, if anything, has changed on campus since 9/11? For example, are there more speakers, more efforts to hire faculty with specialization in the Middle East, etc.? What has changed for your department/project/program/activity since 9/11?
6. In your view, what are the main challenges confronting the teaching and learning of Middle East Studies in the next several years, both in general and on this campus and what can be done to meet these challenges?
7. Do you have any other additional comments?

Phase II Interview Instruments

INTERVIEW QUESTIONS (FORMAL)

Center Director/Administrator

Introduction. Thank you for agreeing to participate in this study. As you know, we are studying area studies centers across the United

States as well as regional and international programming on campuses more generally. Your university is one of six sites participating in this phase of the project. During this site visit, we are focusing on three areas:

- Issues of interdisciplinarity within area studies centers and internationalization on campus more generally.
- The extent to which area studies or related programs may cross traditional boundaries or overlap with one another, including through the development of new geographical or thematic emphases such as the development of Central Asian studies, studies of southern tier countries, or programs such as global studies, security studies, etc.
- The role of area studies centers more generally (specifically those on the Middle East, Russia/Eurasia, and South Asia)—in particular, we wish to contextualize these centers in relation to other efforts on campus that deal with international and global topics—whether those are organized by geographic region or by thematic focus.

Please note that all responses should be related to the last five years unless there is a compelling example otherwise. [Review and have participants sign consent forms.]

Do you have any questions for me before we begin? The first set of questions relate to your center's structure, mission, and role.

I. Center Structure, Mission, and Role

1a: Centers will be asked to provide a copy of their mission statement in advance of the interview. *For those centers that have a mission statement*: When was the mission statement formulated? Is it reflective of how you see/understand the role of the Center on campus? If not, how has the role of the Center changed since the creation of the mission statement? *If the Center* does not *have a mission statement:* How do you describe the mission of your center? How do you understand the role of the Center on campus?

1a-1: What is the scope of your center and is there a specific geographic and/or thematic focus (e.g., specific countries or regions, an emphasis on transition economies, religion, etc.)? When and why was this focus chosen? Has the focus changed in any way over the past five years? If so, in what way/s and why? What gaps would you say exist in the focus (e.g., geographic regions, thematic topics or languages that are not covered adequately)?

1b: Please describe the structure and organization of your center. How does your center relate to and interact with the central administration of the university and its schools, disciplinary departments, and other international studies centers? Who appoints the Center Director and for how long?

1b-1: How do the relationships you just described affect the Center's ability to function in various areas (e.g., institutional support, research agenda, faculty hiring and tenure decisions, representation of various disciplines, student enrollments)? Are there any current plans to alter these institutional relationships in order to affect the way the Center functions? How do these relationships impact your mission, if at all?

1b-2: How much autonomy does the Center have in terms of its finances, curriculum, or other decision making, such as student enrollment and funding? What do you see as the major constraints to this autonomy? What enables it?

1b-3: Does the Center receive funding aside from Title VI? If so, what kinds of funding support the Center? Are there funds or resources that come directly from donors in the regions of study? How would you characterize the Center's relationship with donors?

1b-4: Do you have adequate staff support and student workers at your center? If not, what could be done to alleviate the problem or what could be reorganized? What does the Center need?

1c: What, if anything, has changed on campus over the last five years in response to world events and domestic politics/policies— including 9/11 and related events? For example, how have events affected efforts to hire faculty with specialization in **Middle East/ Russia/Eurasia/South Asia** student enrollments, dissertation topics, course offerings, center speakers, etc.? What has changed for your center, in particular, over this same period? (e.g., have the administrative burdens changed?)

The next set of questions relate to the course offerings more specifically.

II. Center Structure (Course Offerings in Detail)

2a: Are there adequate courses that focus on **Middle East/Russia/ Eurasia/South Asia** to respond to student demand? Are there enough faculty in different disciplines who can advise student dissertations on [**the region**]? To what extent do the various academic disciplines (especially economics, political science, and sociology) offer courses that focus on Middle East/Russia/Eurasia/South Asia? How do these courses relate to your center (i.e. cross-listed, co-taught, etc.)?

2.a-1: Is there sufficient language instruction/training in the languages of the region to meet student demand? If not, what languages are missing from the curriculum? Is there adequate instruction to prepare students to successfully undertake and complete their dissertation research? **If the Center Director and Administrator feel language training is limited**: How does this affect the Center's ability to attract students into the general study of the region? Does this have an impact on your ability to support graduate and PhD research?

Now I would like to turn to questions about interdisciplinarity.

III. Center Interdisciplinarity

3a: Please describe your center's relationship with other academic departments on campus? For example, do you have any involvement in faculty hiring decisions, in the selection of students and the funding of students, in co-sponsoring guest speakers, visiting scholars, etc.? Do you have any influence over departments? Are any classes co-taught with faculty from other departments or are classes cross-listed with other departments? Dissertation committees?

3a-1: To what extent does this relationship vary by department? Which departments have stronger relationships with your center, and why? Does student use of the Center tend to be heavier from certain disciplines? If so, why do you think this is the case? **(Do you see these relationships with academic departments as enhancing or detracting from the teaching and production of knowledge on Middle East/Russia/Eurasia/South Asia on this campus? What impact does that have on promoting your region on your campus?)**

3a-2: Are there any special challenges or difficulties that arise from these relationships with departments (e.g., with regard to institutional support, faculty appointments and tenure decisions, curriculum and course development, research agenda, student enrollments and advising, etc.)?

3b: **For degree granting programs**: What kind of curricular control does the Center have over its own programs and over other degree program curricula? For example, does the Center have a role in selecting the courses that count for degree requirements?

The next few questions focus on your center's relationship with other centers on campus.

IV. The Center's Role vis-à-vis Other Units and Centers

4a: Do you have a relationship with other area studies centers on campus? How would you define this relationship/s? Are there geographic or thematic areas of overlap with other centers? What about with other centers focused on subregional or national areas in *Middle East/Russia/Eurasia/South Asia* and thematic centers, such as religious study centers, conflict/peace study centers, or cross-boundary centers—such as migration or environmental study centers? Do area studies centers here get involved with these centers? Does your center?

4b: Have any new programs or initiatives emerged on campus that focus on Middle East/ Russia/Eurasia/South Asia or related areas? *Note for interviewer: Specifically in the last 5 years.* How did these come about? What has the Center's role been in facilitating the development of these programs and initiatives? In your opinion, do these programs and initiatives add to or detract from the Center? How?

4c: Does the Center engage with other university efforts to establish partnerships in Middle East/Russia/Eurasia/South Asia (e.g., satellite and branch campuses)?

4d: To what degree does your center interact with similar centers at universities across the United States? Are there other forms of outreach with neighboring universities, liberal arts colleges, etc.?

I'd like to turn to a few questions about how the Center relates to international initiatives.

V. The Center's Role in Interfacing with International Initiatives
A. INDIVIDUAL OPPORTUNITIES FOR STUDENTS/FACULTY (OUTBOUND)

5a: What opportunities are available for faculty and students to travel to Middle East/Russia/Eurasia/South Asia for teaching, study, internships, practical training, and/or research? How does the Center facilitate these opportunities, including financially? Have these opportunities diminished or increased within the past five years? If so, how?

5b: Does the Center benefit from these individual exchanges? If so, in what ways? Does the Center track individual student/faculty travel to the region? If so, how?

B. INDIVIDUAL OPPORTUNITIES (INBOUND)

5c: What can you tell me about students from the region on campus? Do they come from one specific region and/or background? How do students from the region interact with your center? How are they recruited, if at all? What sort of support and funding is available to them?

5d: What can you tell me about faculty from the region on campus? Are these faculty affiliated with your center? Are there initiatives to recruit faculty from the region? If so, are you involved with these initiatives?

5e: What other types of foreign visitors does the university host from the region, i.e. visiting scholars, lecturers, foreign dignitaries, etc.? Is the Center engaged in/consulted on such visits? If so: in what ways? What role do these visitors play for your center in particular, and on campus more generally?

5f: In your view, have opportunities to bring foreign students, faculty, and other visitors to campus diminished or increased over the past five years? Why do you think this is?

C. Institutional Opportunities

5g: Does the Center have existing relationships with particular institutions and universities in the region? What types of relationships (e.g., with regard to teaching, research, student and faculty exchanges, material sharing, conferences, etc.)?

Note to interviewer: Please ask for concrete examples.

5g.-1: Please describe your experience in establishing and maintaining these relationships—e.g., particular challenges or difficulties? Particular ways in which they went smoothly or very positively?

The last few questions relate primarily to the future direction of international issues and initiatives here on campus.

VI. Future Directions and Other Issues

6a: How have international initiatives been received by both students and faculty of the Center and the larger university? Does the University recognize the significance of internationalization on campus? In particular, does the university acknowledge the Center's role in coordinating many of these activities? In what ways?

6b: How typical is your center compared to other Middle East/ Russia/Eurasia/South Asia centers that you know—what is unique about your center? How would you say your center differs from other area studies centers on campus?

6c: In your view, what are the main challenges confronting the field of Middle East/Russia/Eurasia/South Asia studies in the next several years, both in general and on this campus? What can be done to meet these challenges?

6d: Does the Center have any specific plans to establish new programs and services or to expand or improve existing ones?

e: If you had more funding, what would you do? For example, in what ways would you expand the Center's programming?

Note to interviewer: At this point, ask other questions specifically related to the Center.

Final Questions

6f: Please make any additional comments you wish about Middle East Russia/Eurasia /South Asia studies either in general or on this campus.

6g: What sort of feedback from this evaluation would be helpful to you? Do you have any specific concerns/questions that should be included in our online survey?

Thank you very much!

Note to interviewer: Assess the extent to which area studies as a paradigm is challenged and questioned. Have recent political events—including, but not limited to, 9/11— reaffirmed or weakened this paradigm?

INTERVIEW QUESTIONS (FORMAL)

Chairs of Sociology, Economics, and Political Science Departments

Introduction. Thank you for agreeing to participate in this study. As you know, we are studying area studies centers across the United States as well as regional and international programming on campuses more generally. Your university is one of six sites participating in this phase of the project. During this site visit, we are focusing on three areas:

- Issues of interdisciplinarity within area studies centers and internationalization on campus more generally.
- The extent to which area studies or related programs may cross traditional boundaries or overlap with one another, including through the development of new geographical or thematic emphases such as the development of Central Asian studies, studies of southern tier countries, or programs such as global studies, security studies, etc.
- The role of area studies centers more generally (specifically those on the Middle East, Russia/Eurasia, and South Asia)—in particular, we wish to contextualize these centers in relation to other efforts on campus which deal with international and global topics—whether those are organized by geographic region or by thematic focus.

[Review and have participants sign consent form.]

Do you have any questions for me before we begin?

1. How would you characterize the main trends within your discipline in regards to international issues?

2. What kinds of challenges, if any, are involved with combining a regional specialization with disciplinary training in **sociology/ economics/political science**? Are there course offerings in this department focused on international topics? Are there research projects focused on international topics, and if so, what kind?

2a: Are there constraints or barriers for faculty who wish to engage in international research? For example, can faculty members find adequate time to study new languages? Is there support for faculty members who wish to travel overseas for research or study?

3. How many faculty members are there in this department whose research focuses on international topics? Has this number changed in the recent past?

4. What do you know about your graduate students' relationship with area studies centers (meaning those students who are working on international topics)? Do the Centers provide resources, faculty expertise, etc. to these students? Are there additional resources that the students require that these centers do not provide?

5. In your view, to what extent does the University prioritize international issues? Does this impact your ability to recruit and maintain students and faculty interested in international issues?

6. How would you characterize area studies centers on this campus? Are they a resource to the work of your department? If so, how? If not, why not?

Thank you!

INTERVIEW QUESTIONS (FORMAL)

Provost or International Administrator

Introduction: Thank you for agreeing to participate in this study. As you know, we are studying area studies centers across the United States as well as regional and international programming on campuses more generally. Your university is one of six sites participating in this phase of the project. During this site visit, we are focusing on three areas:

- Issues of interdisciplinarity within area studies centers and internationalization on campus more generally.
- The extent to which area studies or related programs may cross traditional boundaries or overlap with one another, including

through the development of new geographical or thematic emphases such as the development of Central Asian studies, studies of southern tier countries, or programs such as global studies, security studies, etc.

- The role of area studies centers more generally (specifically those on the Middle East, Russia/Eurasia, and South Asia)—in particular, we wish to contextualize these centers in relation to other efforts on campus which deal with international and global topics—whether those are organized by geographic region or by thematic focus.

[Review and have participants sign consent form.]

Do you have any questions for me before we begin?
1. How is teaching and research on world regions and/or international programming structured on campus (i.e., through centers, institutes, departments, special programs, etc.)? How would you say this structure has changed over the past five years, if at all (e.g., new programs or degrees, new funding streams, new centers)? Why have these changes occurred? (*If no mention of 9/11 or Iraq war, etc., ask about this.*) How do your campus programs and priorities in terms of regional and international activities differ from other university campuses?
1.a: What is your role in overseeing these programs, and who else is involved in oversight? At the university level, are there any particular world regions or international initiatives that are prioritized over others and if so, what is the reason for these priorities (e.g., student demand, faculty hires, availability of funding, university partnerships, etc.)?
2. How would you describe the role of area studies centers on campus (e.g., offering degrees, supporting disciplinary training, etc.)? What is the relationship among area studies centers in terms of international programming as you described to me more generally? *If new programs or initiatives were mentioned in Question 1: how integral have area studies centers been in creating and implementing the new programs/initiatives that you mentioned? Has there been any resistance between area studies centers and the new programs to work together?*
2.a Our study is particularly interested in area studies centers that focus on the Middle East, Russia/Eurasia, and South Asia; how important would you rate these centers individually or collectively for the university? What would this university look like without the centers?
2.b: What is this office's relationship with area studies centers? Who appoints the directors of the centers, and for what period of time? What

level of expertise does the university have in relation to the three regions on which we are focused? Does any one or do all of these regions constitute a priority for university instruction? If so, why?

3. How would you describe the relationship between the disciplines and the area studies centers on this campus? One of the reasons we are interested in these questions is because, as you may know, area studies centers have traditionally been stronger in the humanities than in the social sciences. Specifically, we see fewer students from political science, sociology, and economics working on regions such as the Middle East, Russia/Eurasia, and South Asia, as compared to students from religion, history, and literature. Do you think this is an accurate characterization of this campus? If so, do you see anything specific at this university that contributes to this trend? In other words, in the social sciences, are there structural or other deterrents to students' engagement with international topics? Do you see this imbalance as a problem, and if so, is this a problem that needs to be addressed at the university level or on a nationwide level?

3.a: What types of requests/complaints do you hear from departmental faculty, administrators, or students in terms of their interaction with area studies centers and with the availability of area studies or international programming on campus more broadly?

4. What kinds of constraints or barriers do you face in your efforts to develop or expand international initiatives or regional programming on this campus? What are some of the main challenges facing area studies, in particular, now and in the near future, both on this campus and in general? What can be done to meet these challenges? What might this university look like if these restraints no longer existed?

What additional comments would you like to make concerning one or more of the three area studies centers that we are discussing, or anything else we have discussed?

Thank you very much!

Notes to interviewer: Ask specifically about boundary crossing if this does not come up in the context of Questions 1 and 2.

Please be sure to mention the second set of site visits, scheduled for fall 2007 and spring 2008 semesters at this stage in the fieldwork process.

Notes to Introduction

1. "Notice Inviting Applications for New Awards for Fiscal Year (FY) 2004," *Federal Register* 68: no. 165 (Tuesday 26 August 2003):51261–51263.
2. Text adapted and quoted from the 2003 grant proposal "Internationalization and Inter-disciplinarity: An Evaluation of Title VI Middle East Studies Centers" to the International Research & Studies Program of the US Department of Education. Principal Investigator Seteney Shami. Internal document, SSRC.
3. See Cynthia Miller-Idriss, *Blood and Culture: Youth, Right-Wing Extremism, and National Belonging in Contemporary Germany* (Durham, NC: Duke University Press, 2009).
4. Mitchell L. Stevens, *Creating a Class: College Admissions and the Education of Elites* (Cambridge, MA: Harvard University Press, 2007); Mitchell L. Stevens, Elizabeth A. Armstrong, and Richard Arum, "Sieve, Incubator, Temple, Hub: Empirical and Theoretical Advances in the Sociology of Higher Education," *Annual Review of Sociology* 34 (2008):127–151.
5. More information on the larger project may be found at ssrc.org /producingknowledgeworldregions.
6. Seteney Shami and Cynthia Miller-Idriss, *Middle East Studies for the New Millennium: Infrastructures of Knowledge* (New York: New York University Press, 2016).
7. See the appendix for interview instruments.

Chapter 1: The World in US Universities

1. We are hardly the first to ask such questions. We are indebted especially to those in the Stanford school of education and world society. See, for example, David John Frank and Jay Gabler, *Reconstructing the University: Worldwide Shifts in Academia in the Twentieth Century* (Stanford, CA: Stanford University Press, 2006). Our work differs in its focus on how universities organize the daily work of scholarship and teaching—rather than changes in the curricular corpus.

2. Paul DiMaggio, "Culture and Cognition," *Annual Review of Sociology* 23 (1997): 263–287; quotation on p. 269.

3. The claims of this paragraph directly parallel those in Mitchell L. Stevens, *Kingdom of Children: Culture and Controversy in the Homeschooling Movement* (Princeton: Princeton University Press, 2001), p. 109.

4. Geneviève Zubrzycki, *The Crosses of Auschwitz: Nationalism and Religion in Post-Communist Poland* (Chicago: University of Chicago Press, 2006), pp. xi–xiii. A related theoretical statement is Elisabeth S. Clemens, "Toward a Historicized Sociology: Theorizing Events, Processes, and Emergence," *Annual Review of Sociology* 33 (2007):527–549.

5. The signal treatise is Edward Said, *Orientalism* (New York: Vintage Books, 1978). The subsequent literatures, sometimes subsumed under the broad banner of postcolonial theory, are vast.

6. John Willinsky, *Learning to Divide the World: Education at Empire's End* (Minneapolis: University of Minnesota Press, 1998), p. 57.

7. David F. Labaree, "The Power of the Parochial in Shaping the American System of Higher Education," in Paul Smeyers and Marc Depaepe (eds.), *Educational Research: Institutional Spaces of Educational Research* (Dordrecht: Springer, 2013), pp. 31–46.

8. Michael D. Kennedy and Miguel A. Centeno, "Internationalism and Global Transformations in American Sociology," in Craig Calhoun (ed.), *Sociology in America: A History* (Chicago: University of Chicago Press, 2007), pp. 666–712. Quote is from p. 669. Kennedy and Centeno credit Immanuel Wallerstein for this idea. See Wallerstein's "The Heritage of Sociology: The Promise of Social Science," in Immanuel Wallerstein, *The End of the World as We Know It: Social Science for the Twenty-First Century* (Minneapolis: University of Minnesota Press, 1999), pp. 220–551.

9. See discussion and citations in Chapter 3.

10. Edward Said, "Jane Austen and Empire," in Julie Rivkin and Michael Ryan (eds.), *Literary Theory: An Anthology*, 2nd ed. (Oxford: Blackwell, 2004 [1998]), pp. 1112–1125.

11. Seymour Martin Lipset, *The First New Nation: The United States in Historical and Comparative Perspective* (New Brunswick, NJ: Transaction Publishers, 2003 [1963]).

12. Peter Worsely, *The Three Worlds: Culture and World Development* (Chicago: University of Chicago Press, 1984).

13. Nils Gilman, *Mandarins of the Future: Modernization Theory in Cold War America* (Baltimore: The Johns Hopkins University Press, 2003).

14. Harvard, Yale, and Princeton had early ambitions for producing a national leadership class. See Jerome Karabel, *The Chosen: The Hidden History of Admission and Exclusion at Harvard, Yale, and Princeton* (New York: Houghton Mifflin, 2005). Also Peter Dobkin Hall, *The Organization of American Culture, 1700–1900: Private Institutions, Elites, and the Origins of American Nationality* (New York: New York University Press, 1982).

15. See Suzanne Mettler, *From Soldiers to Citizens: The GI Bill and the Making of the Greatest Generation* (New York: Oxford University Press, 2005).

16. This section relies on a wealth of secondary scholarship on the central role of US higher education in the Cold War effort of the twentieth century. We call out two early texts here and cite additional scholarship in Chapter 2. Daniel Lee Kleinman, *Politics on the Endless Frontier: Postwar Research Policy in the United States* (Durham, NC: Duke University Press, 1995); Rebecca S. Lowen, *Creating the Cold War University: The Transformation of Stanford* (Berkeley: University of California Press, 1997).

17. George Steinmetz, "Preface," in George Steinmetz (ed.), *Sociology and Empire: The Imperial Entanglements of a Discipline* (Durham, NC: Duke University Press, 2013), pp. ix–xvi. Quote is from p. xiii.

18. Brian Balogh, *A Government Out of Sight: The Mystery of National Authority in Nineteenth Century America* (Cambridge: Cambridge University Press, 2009). Also Loss, *Between Citizens and the State: The Politics of American Higher Education in the Twentieth Century* (Princeton: Princeton University Press, 2012). Inheriting Balogh's insight, Loss refers to US higher education in the twentieth century as a "parastate."

19. C. Wright Mills, *The Sociological Imagination* (New York: Oxford University Press, 1959), p. 106. See also Steinmetz, Preface, p. xii.

20. Andrew Abbott and James T. Sparrow, "Hot War, Cold War: The Structures of Sociological Action, 1940–1955," in Craig Calhoun (ed.), *Sociology in America: A History* (Chicago: University of Chicago Press, 2007), pp. 281–313.

21. On the historical rise of the ideal of objectivity in the applied social sciences, see Lisa Anderson, *Pursuing Truth, Exercising Power: Social Science and Public Policy in the Twenty-First Century* (New York: Columbia University Press, 2003). On the prestige of quantitative data sets in social science see Wendy Nelson Espeland and Mitchell L. Stevens, "A Sociology of Quantification," *European Journal of Sociology* XLIX (2008):401– 436.

22. Engerman, *Know Your Enemy*, p. 2. Launched with significant support from the US government and from the Rockefeller Foundation, Soviet studies emerged during the closing years of World War II as the first domain of area studies in the service of national security, assembling scholars from traditional disciplines in a new form of interdisciplinary enterprise "oriented around practical problems rather than disciplinary expectations and to training practical experts to work in government agencies" (p. 3). Perhaps most notably, Russian Studies programs focused heavily on the humanities, emphasizing "linguistic competence and cultural knowledge," sending not only social scientists, but also large numbers of historians and humanists to study abroad (p. 4). Other foundations, such as the Carnegie Corporation and Ford, quickly followed Rockefeller's lead, pouring millions of dollars into support for area studies programming at US universities. Ford became particularly invested, and "quickly dwarfed all public and private funding sources for international studies in the United States" (p. 41).

23. Engerman, *Know Your Enemy*, p. 44, citing Alex Leighton, *Human Relations in a Changing World: Observations on the Use of the Social Sciences* (New York, 1949), 43, 44 and passim.

24. Loss, *Between Citizens and the State*, pp. 121–164.
25. Kennedy and Centeno, "Internationalism and Global Transformations," p. 678.
26. See our longer discussion and additional citations in Chapter 2.
27. George Steinmetz, "American Sociology before and after World War II: The (Temporary) Settling of a Disciplinary Field," in Craig Calhoun (ed.), *Sociology in America: A History* (Chicago: University of Chicago Press, 2007), pp. 314–366.
28. Björn Wittrock, "History and Sociology: Transmutations of Historical Reasoning in the Social Sciences," in Peter Hedström and Björn Wittrock (eds.), *Frontiers of Sociology*. Annals of the International Institute of Sociology, Vol. 11 (Boston: Brill, 2009), pp. 77–112. Quote is from p. 89.
29. Kennedy and Centeno, "Internationalism and Global Transformations," p. 681.
30. Gilman, *Mandarins of the Future*.
31. "American Sociology before and after World War II: The (Temporary) Settling of a Disciplinary Field," in Craig Calhoun (ed.), *Sociology in America: A History* (Chicago: University of Chicago Press, 2007), pp. 314–366. See also Immanuel Wallerstein, "Unintended Consequences of Cold War Area Studies;" also "1968, Revolution in the World-System," in Immanuel Wallerstein, *Geopolitics and Geoculture: Essays on the Changing World-System* (Cambridge: Cambridge University Press, 1991), pp. 65–83.
32. See, for example, Immanuel Wallerstein, *The Politics of the World Economy: The States, the Movements, and the Civilizations* (Cambridge: Cambridge University Press, 1984).
33. For a critical review see Arjun Appadurai, *Modernity at Large: Cultural Dynamics of Modernity* (Minneapolis: University of Minnesota Press, 1996). James C. Scott, *Seeing Like a State: How Certain Schemes to Improve the Human Condition Have Failed* (New Haven, CT: Yale University Press, 1998). For an incisive sociology of the development project see Jocelyn Viterna and Cassandra Robertson, "New Directions in the Sociology of Development," *Annual Review of Sociology* 41(2015):243–269. Modernization theory continues to inspire debate. See, for example, the collection of essays edited by David Palumbo-Liu, Bruce Robbins, and Nirvana Tanoukhi, *Immanuel Wallerstein and the Problem of the World: System, Scale, Culture* (Durham, NC: Duke University Press, 2011).
34. For an overview of scholarship on this epochal shift in the organization of US higher education see Mitchell L. Stevens and Ben Gebre-Medhin, "Association, Service, Market: Higher Education in American Political Development," *Annual Review of Sociology* 42 (2016):121–124. Recent laments about static or declining funding of basic research by government agencies include the American Academy of Arts & Sciences, *Restoring the Foundation: The Vital Role of Research in Preserving the American Dream* (Cambridge, MA: American Academy of Arts and Sciences, 2014); also Jonathan R. Cole, *The Great American University: Its Rise to Preeminence, Its Indispensable National Role, and Why It Must Be Protected* (New York: Public Affairs, 2009).

35. Isaac Martin, *The Permanent Tax Revolt: How the Property Tax Transformed American Politics* (Stanford, CA: Stanford University Press, 2008).
36. For a review of these changes at the state-government level, see Patricia A. Gumport, "Academic Restructuring: Organizational Change and Institutional Imperatives," *Higher Education* 39 (2000):67–91.
37. For a succinct review see Steven Brint, "Creating the Future: 'New Directions in American Research Universities," *Minerva* 43 (2005):23–50.
38. Elizabeth Popp Berman, *Creating the Market University: How Academic Science Became an Economic Engine* (Princeton: Princeton University Press, 2012).
39. Elizabeth A. Armstrong and Laura T. Hamilton, *Paying for the Party: How College Maintains Inequality* (Cambridge, MA: Harvard University Press, 2013).
40. Ozan Jaquette and Bradley R. Curs, "Creating the Out-of-State University: Do Public Universities Increase Enrollments in Response to Declining State Appropriations?" *Research in Higher Education* 56 (2015):535–565; John Bound, B Braga, G Khanna, and Sarah Turner, "A Passage to America: University Funding and International Students," University of Michigan-Ann Arbor, working paper (2015).
41. On rising college costs generally see Ronald G. Ehrenberg, *Tuition Rising: Why College Costs So Much* (Cambridge, MA: Harvard University Press, 2002); also Sara Goldrick-Rab, *Paying the Price: College Costs, Financial Aid, and the Betrayal of the American Dream* (Chicago: University of Chicago Press, 2016).
42. For a useful summary of US higher education finance in the post–World War II era see William Zumeta, David W. Brenneman, Patrick M. Callan, and Joni E. Finney, *Financing American Higher Education in the Era of Globalization* (Cambridge, MA: Harvard University Press, 2012). For a critical narrative account of the changing financial structure of elite higher education in particular, see David Kirp's *Shakespeare, Einstein, and the Bottom Line: The Marketing of Higher Education* (Cambridge, MA: Harvard University Press, 2003).
43. For a succinct review of this vast literature see Saskia Sassen, *Cities in a World Economy,* 4th ed. (Los Angeles: Sage, 2012); also Neil Brenner, *New State Spaces: Urban Governance and the Rescaling of Statehood* (New York: Oxford University Press, 2004).
44. A touchstone volume for anthropology and the humanistic social sciences more broadly was James G. Clifford and George E. Marcus, *Writing Culture: The Poetics and Politics of Ethnography* (Berkeley: University of California Press, 1986).
45. Martin W. Lewis and Kären Wigen, *The Myth of Continents: A Critique of Metageography* (Berkeley: University of California Press, 1997).
46. See, for example, Saskia Sassen, *Territory, Authority, Rights: From Medieval to Global Assemblages* (Princeton: Princeton University Press, 2006); James Clifford, *Routes: Travel and Translation in the Late Twentieth Century* (Cambridge, MA: Harvard University Press, 1997).
47. See, for example, Arjun Appadurai, *The Future as Cultural Fact: Essays on the Global Condition* (New York: Verso Press, 2013); Seyla Benhabib,

The Claims of Culture: Equality and Diversity in the Global Era (Princeton: Princeton University Press, 2002); Michael D. Kennedy, *Globalizing Knowledge: Intellectuals, Universities and Publics in Transformation* (Stanford, CA: Stanford University Press, 2014). For an earlier discussion of similar issues, see Sandra Harding, *Whose Science: Whose Knowledge? Thinking from Women's Lives,* especially chapters 8 and 9 (Ithaca, NY: Cornell University Press, 1991).

48. This insight is inspired by a parallel one on K–12 US schools in David Tyack and Larry Cuban, *Tinkering toward Utopia: A Century of Public School Reform* (Cambridge, MA: Harvard University Press, 1997).

49. We thank Jerry Jacobs for the metaphor.

50. For a provocative recent statement see David Labaree, *A Perfect Mess: The Unlikely Ascendancy of American Higher Education* (Chicago: University of Chicago Press, 2017). Classic statements on the complexity and anarchy of US universities include Clark Kerr, *The Uses of the University* (Cambridge, MA: Harvard University Press, 2001 [1963]), and Michael D. Cohen, James G. March, and Johan P. Olsen, "A Garbage Can Model of Organizational Choice," *Administrative Science Quarterly* 17 (1972):1–25.

Chapter 2: What Is Area Studies?

1. Robert Lowie, *Primitive Society* (New York: Boni & Liveright, 1920), p. 441.

2. Andrew Abbott *Chaos of Disciplines* (Chicago: University of Chicago Press, 2001). We take up this phenomenon more directly in Chapter 3.

3. Dorothy Ross, *The Origins of American Social Science* (Cambridge: Cambridge University Press, 1991).

4. Scott Frickel and Neil Gross, "A General Theory of Scientific/Intellectual Movements," *American Journal of Sociology* 70 (2005):204–232. Quote is from p. 206.

5. See especially Michael E. Latham, *Modernization as Ideology: American Social Science and "Nation Building" in the Kennedy Era* (Chapel Hill: University of North Carolina Press, 2000); Nils Gilman, *Mandarins of the Future: Modernization Theory in Cold War America* (Baltimore: The Johns Hopkins University Press, 2003); Margaret O'Mara, *Cities of Knowledge: Cold War Science and the Search for the Next Silicon Valley* (Princeton: Princeton University Press, 2005); Christopher P. Loss, *Between Citizens and the State: The Politics of American Higher Education in the Twentieth Century* (Princeton: Princeton University Press, 2012); Joel Isaac, *Working Knowledge: Making the Human Sciences from Parsons to Kuhn* (Cambridge, MA: Harvard University Press, 2012).

6. Loss, *Between Citizens and the State.* Also Christopher P. Loss, "'The most wonderful thing has happened to me in the army': Psychology, Citizenship, and American Higher Education in World War II," *The Journal of American History* 92 (2005):864–891.

7. Just how the area studies project has coevolved with disciplinary inquiry has inspired its own genre of lively debate, to which our own analyses in subse-

quent chapters contribute. For a fuller range of positions see also Richard J. Samuels and Myron Weiner (eds.), *The Political Culture of Foreign Area and International Studies: Essays in Honor of Lucien W. Pye* (New York: Brassey's, 1992); "Moderated Discussion: Comparative Education, Area Studies, and the Disciplines," *Comparative Education Review* 50 (2006):125–148.

8. Kenton W. Worchester, *Social Science Research Council, 1923–1998* (New York: Social Science Research Council, 2001).

9. Here we depart somewhat from Zachary Lockman's careful account of area studies in *Field Notes: The Making of Middle East Studies in the United States* (Stanford, CA: Stanford University Press, 2016). Whereas Lockman emphasizes the continuity of regional inquiry on the Middle East from the civilizational inquiry through the Cold War period, for our purposes it is important to note how the modernization project essentially transformed social science inquiry on regions, placing that inquiry directly in the service of the federal government.

10. Gilman, *Mandarins of the Future*, p. 113. See Isaac, *Working Knowledge*, on Harvard specifically.

11. On Sovietology and the Cold War see David Engerman, *Know Your Enemy: The Rise and Fall of America's Soviet Experts* (New York: Oxford University Press, 2006).

12. Ode Arne Westad, *The Global Cold War* (Cambridge: Cambridge University Press, 2007).

13. Signal texts of modernization theory include W. W. Rostow, *The Stages of Economic Growth: A Non-Communist Manifesto* (Cambridge: Cambridge University Press, 1960); D. Lerner, *The Passing of Traditional Society: Modernizing the Middle East* (Glencoe, IL: Free Press, 1958); David E. Apter, *The Politics of Modernization* (Chicago: University of Chicago Press, 1965).

14. Latham, *Modernization as Ideology*, p. 209.

15. A succinct overview of the history of area studies is Immanuel Wallerstein, "The Unintended Consequences of Cold War Area Studies," in Andre Schiffrin (ed.), *The Cold War and the University: Toward and Intellectual History of the Postwar Years* (New York: The New Press, 1997), pp. 195–232. For a detailed history of Title VI, see Nancy L. Ruther, *Barely There, Powerfully Present: Thirty Years of U.S. Policy on International Higher Education* (London and New York: Routledge, 2002).

16. Robert A. McCaughey, *International Studies and Academic Enterprise: A Chapter in the Enclosure of American Learning* (New York: Columbia University Press, 1984).

17. Craig Calhoun, "Renewing International Studies," in David S. Wiley and Robert S. Glew (eds.), *International and Language Education for a Global Future* (East Lansing: Michigan State University Press, 2010), pp. 227–254. Also Cynthia Miller-Idriss and Elizabeth Anderson Worden, "Internationalisation in US Higher Education: Studying the Middle East in the American University," *Globalisation, Societies and Education*, 8 (2010):393–409.

18. Seymour Martin Lipset, *The First New Nation: The United States in Historical and Comparative Perspective* (New York: Basic Books, 1963).

19. For this section we are indebted to an essay by Srirupa Roy. "Debates on Area Studies" (New York: Social Science Research Council, n.d.). Also Vicente L. Rafael, "The Cultures of Area Studies in the United States," *Social Text* 41(1994): 91–111.

20. Loren Graham and Jean-Michel Kantor, "'Soft' Area Studies versus 'Hard' Social Science: A False Opposition," *Slavic Review* 66 (2007):1–19.

21. Mark Tessler, Jodi Nachtwey, and Anne Banda, "Introduction: The Area Studies Controversy," in Tessler, Mark (ed.), with Jody Nachtway and Anne Banda, *Area Studies and Social Science: Strategies for Understanding Middle East Politics* (Bloomington: Indiana University Press, 1999), pp. vii–xxi.

22. John Lie, "Asian Studies/Global Studies: Transcending Area Studies and Social Sciences," *Cross-Currents: East Asian History and Culture Review* 2 (2012):5.

23. For a statement regarding the geographical chauvinism of the social sciences see Raewyn Connell, "Northern Theory: The Political Geography of General Social Theory," *Theory and Society* 35(2006):237–264.

24. Mark Solovey, "Project Camelot and the 1960s Epistemological Revolution: Rethinking the Politics-Patronage-Social Science Nexus." *Social Studies of Science* 31(2001):171–206.

25. Seteney Shami and Marcial Godoy-Anativia, "Area Studies and the Decade after 9/11," in Shami, Seteney and Cynthia Miller-Idriss (eds.), *Middle East Studies for the New Millenium: Infrastructures of Knowledge* (New York: NYU Press, 2016), pp. 351–374.

26. See the collection edited by Seteney Shami and Cynthia Miller-Idriss, *Middle East Studies for the New Millennium: Infrastructures of Knowledge* (New York: NYU Press, 2016).

27. Ruble, Blair A. Ruble, Foreword, in Daniel Orlovsky, *Beyond Soviet Studies* (Washington, DC: The Woodrow Wilson Center Press, 1995), pp. ix–xi.

28. Orlovsky (ed.), *Beyond Soviet Studies*, p. 1.

29. Catherine Doughty, "Language Competence, Performance, Proficiency, and Certification: Current Status and New Directions," in David Wiley and Robert Glew (eds.), *International and Language Education for a Global Future: Fifty Years of U.S. Title VI and Fulbright-Hays Programs* (East Lansing: Michigan State University Press, 2010), pp. 111–135. Also Elaine E. Tarone, "The Impact of Fifty Years of Title VI on Language Learning in the United States," pp. 71–88 in the same volume.

30. Cynthia Miller-Idriss, "Going Global: How U.S. K–16 Education Is Shaped by the 'Rest' of the World," in Christopher P. Loss and Patrick McGuinn (eds.), The Convergence of K-12 and Higher Education: Policies and Programs in a Changing Era (Cambridge, MA: Harvard Education Press, 2016), pp. 197–214.

31. Mary Ellen O'Connell and Janet L. Norwood (eds.), *International Education and Foreign Language: Keys to Securing America's Future* (Washington, DC: The National Research Council, National Academies Press, 2007).

32. David S. Wiley, "Introduction: Seeking Global Competence through the Title VI and Fulbright-Hays Acts," in David S. Wiley and Robert S. Glew (eds.), *International and Language Education for a Global Future: Fifty Years*

of U.S. Title VI and Fulbright-Hays Programs (East Lansing: Michigan State University Press, 2010), pp. 1–16. The quote is from p. 11.

33. Jonathan Friedman and Cynthia Miller-Idriss, "Gateways and Guest-Homes: How Area Studies Centers Serve as Arbiters of Scholarly Mobility," in Bernhard Streitweiser (ed.), *Internationalization of Higher Education and Global Mobility.* (Oxford, UK: Symposium Books, 2014), pp. 151–168.

34. Jonathan Friedman and Elizabeth A. Worden, "Creating Interdisciplinary Space on Campus: Lessons from US Area Studies Centers," *Higher Education Research and Development* 35 (2016):129–141. Other research supports the assertion of a relationship between physical propinquity and scholarly productivity; see Felichism W. Kabo, Natalie Cotton-Nessler, Yongha Hwang, Margaret C. Levenstein, and Jason Owen-Smith, "Proximity Effects on the Dynamics and Outcomes of Scientific Collaborations," *Research Policy* 43(2014):1469–1485.

35. Friedman and Worden, p. 137. For a statement of the relationship between academic space and status generally see Mitchell L. Stevens, "The Space of SCANCOR," *Nordiske Organisasjonsstudier* 4 (2013):51–54.

36. Immanuel Wallerstein, *Open the Social Sciences: Report of the Gulbenkian Commission on the Restructuring of the Social Sciences* (Stanford, CA: Stanford University Press, 1996). Quotes are from pp. 36 and 38.

37. "The Unintended Consequences of Cold War Area Studies," in Noam Chomsky et al. (eds.), *The Cold War and the University: Toward an Intellectual History of the Postwar Years* (New York: The New Press, 1997), pp. 195–231; also Lockman, *Field Notes.*

38. Quote from Veronica Boix Mansilla, Michèle Lamont, and Kyoko Sato, "Shared Cognitive-Emotional-Interactional Platforms: Markers and Conditions for Successful Interdisciplinary Collaborations." *Science, Technology and Human Values* 41(2016): 571–612. The quote is from p. 572. A fascinating literature of quantitative studies seeks to assess predictors and catalysts of interdisciplinary scholarship. See, for example, Craig M. Rawlings, Daniel A. McFarland, Linus Dahlander, and Dan Wang, "Streams of Thought: Knowledge Flows and Intellectual Cohesion in a Multidisciplinary Era," *Social Forces* 93 (2015):1687–1722; Linus Dahlander and Daniel A. McFarland, "Ties that Last: Tie Formation and Persistence in Research Collaborations over Time," *Administrative Science Quarterly* 58 (2013):69–110.

Chapter 3: Departments and Not-Departments

1. The implications of academic management for institutional prestige have been deftly recognized by Emily J. Levine, "Baltimore Teaches, Göttingen Learns: Cooperation, Competition, and the Research University," *American Historical Review* 121 (June):780–823.

2. For a concise review see Charles Camic, Neil Gross, and Michèle Lamont, "The Study of Social Knowledge Making," in Charles Camic, Neil Gross, and Michèle Lamont, *Social Knowledge in the Making* (Chicago: University of Chicago Press, 2011), pp. 1–40.

3. For a comparative study of knowledge production in physics and biology, see Karin Knorr Cetina, *Epistemic Cultures: How Scientists Make Knowledge* (Cambridge, MA: Harvard University Press, 1999).
4. Andrew Abbott, *Chaos of Disciplines* (Chicago: University of Chicago Press, 2001). An intriguing parallel to our own analysis is intellectual historian Joel Isaac's study of the social sciences at Harvard University in the middle decades of the twentieth century, *Working Knowledge: Making the Human Sciences from Parsons to Kuhn* (Cambridge, MA: Harvard University Press, 2012).
5. Emily J. Levine, "Baltimore Teaches, Göttingen Learns: Cooperation, Competition, and the Research University," *American Historical Review* 121 (June):780–823.
6. In addition to Abbott's own treatment in 2001, the rich narrative history of US higher education includes Laurence R. Veysey, *The Emergence of the American University* (Chicago: University of Chicago Press, 1965); David O. Levine, *The American College and Culture of Aspiration, 1915–1940* (Ithaca, NY: Cornell University Press, 1986). Christopher J. Lucas, *American Higher Education: A History* (New York: St. Martin's Press, 1994); John R. Thelin, *A History of American Higher Education* (Baltimore: The Johns Hopkins University Press, 2011). On the political dynamics of the funding of public universities, see Charles T. Clotfelter, *Big-Time Sports in American Universities* (New York: Cambridge University Press, 2011).
7. See Burton J. Bledstein, *The Culture of Professionalism: The Middle Class and the Development of Higher Education in America* (New York: W. W. Norton, 1978); also Harold S. Wechsler, *The Qualified Student: A History of Selective College Admission in America* (New York: John Wiley & Sons, 1977).
8. Again it is not coincidental that the national disciplinary associations for sociology, economics, history, political science, modern languages and others emerged at the same time as the development of the college major. See Stephen Ellingson, "The Emergence and Institutionalization of the Major-Minor Curriculum, 1870–1910" (Department of Sociology, University of Chicago, 1996); also Cristobal Young, "The Emergence of Sociology from Political Economy in the United States: 1880–1940," *Journal of the History of the Behavioral Sciences* 45 (2009):91–116.
9. Abbott (*Chaos of Disciplines*) describes this elegantly in chapter 5, "The Context of Disciplines," pp. 121–153.
10. Abbott, *Chaos of Disciplines*, p. 49.
11. On academic rankings as discipline and control mechanisms see Wendy Nelson Espeland and Michael Sauder, *Engines of Anxiety: Academic Rankings, Reputation, and Accountability* (New York: Russell Sage Foundation, 2016).
12. See, for example, Jerry A. Jacobs, *In Defense of Disciplines: Interdisciplinarity and Specialization in the Research University* (Chicago: University of Chicago Press, 2013), whose core argument we take up in chapter 3. We read Michèle Lamont's *How Professors Think: Inside the Curious World of Academic Judgment* (Cambridge, MA: Harvard University Press, 2009) as harmonious with Abbott's work as well.
13. Modern Language Association, *Report of the MLA Task Force on Doctoral Study on Modern Language and Literature*, 2014 (May).

14. On the centrality of doctoral training to the academic prestige system, see Julie R. Posselt, *Inside Graduate Admissions: Merit, Diversity, and Faculty Gatekeeping* (Cambridge, MA: Harvard University Press, 2016).

15. The scope of faculty governance has become newly problematic as the basic financial structure of US higher education continues to be in flux. See William G. Bowen and Eugene M. Tobin, *The Locus of Authority: The Evolution of Faculty Roles in the Governance of Higher Education* (Princeton: Princeton University Press, 2015). How those who are empowered by the inherited governance structure we and Abbott describe will respond to these new critiques remains an open question—though the steady rise of the not-department form and steady decline in the proportion of faculty in tenure-line appointments together suggest a secular diminishment of the purview of faculty authority.

16. Andrew Abbott, "Status and Status Strain in the Professions," *American Journal of Sociology* 86 (1981):815–835.

17. Although investigating it fully is beyond the scope of this inquiry, our work strongly suggests a coevolution of departments and not-departments. Our hypothesis would be that departments require buffers at their interstices and peripheries to manage the intellectual and political contradictions inherent in the disciplinary system. For classic works on the concept of core buffering, see James G. March and Herbert Simon, *Organizations* (New York: John Wiley & Sons, 1958). Also James D. Thompson, *Organizations in Action* (New York: McGraw-Hill, 1967). See also Andrew Abbott's "Things of Boundaries," *Social Research* 62 (1995):857–882, which makes an intriguing argument about how boundaries constitute new social entities. Not-departments might appropriately be viewed as organizational technologies for turning boundaries (between disciplines, between disciplines and publics) into things.

18. Here we both learn and depart from a prescient analysis by Susan Biancani, Daniel A. McFarland, and Linus Dahlander, "The Semiformal Organization," *Organization Science* 25 (2014):1306–1324, based on a study of academic units that are not departments at Stanford University. Our own inquiry indicates that many not-departments are important units of formal organization with clear boundaries, memberships, revenue streams, and reporting structures.

19. See Zachary Lockman, *Field Notes: The Making of Middle East Studies in the United States* (Stanford, CA: Stanford University Press, 2016).

20. In this sense Title VI centers are "boundary organizations," enabling universities and their personnel to manage relationships with consequential networks beyond the academy. On boundary organizations see Siobhán O'Mahoney and Beth A. Bechky, "Boundary Organizations: Enabling Collaboration Among Unexpected Allies." *Administrative Science Quarterly* 53 (2008):422–459.

21. In *How Professors Think*, Lamont explains the volume of evaluative work in the US academy as a function of the massive scale of the US academic world and the steady rationalization of its reward distribution.

22. Joshua Guetzkow, Michèle Lamont, and Grégoire Mallard, "What Is Originality in the Social Sciences and the Humanities?" *American Sociological Review* 69 (2004):190–212.

23. See, for example, Neil Gross, *Richard Rorty: The Making of an American Philosopher* (Chicago: University of Chicago Press, 2008).

24. Detailed treatments of academic competition include Richard Whitley, *The Intellectual and Social Organization of the Sciences* (Oxford: Clarendon Press, 1984); and Pierre Bourdieu (trans. Peter Collier), *Homo Academicus* (Cambridge, MA: Polity Press, 1988).

25. Recent synoptic treatments of identity and multiplicity include Neil Fligstein and Doug McAdam, *A Theory of Fields* (New York: Oxford University Press, 2012); John F. Padgett and Walter J. Powell, *The Emergence of Organizations and Markets* (Princeton: Princeton Univerity Press, 2012).

Chapter 4: Stone Soup

1. A classic treatise on this enduring metaphor of intellectual life is Diana Crane, *Invisible Colleges: Diffusion of Knowledge in Scientific Communities* (Chicago: University of Chicago Press, 1972).

2. We are referring here to the extensive literature on individual and group behavior that also flies under the banner of rational choice. Benchmark works of sociological theory in this tradition are James S. Coleman, *Foundations of Social Theory* (Cambridge, MA: Harvard University Press, 1990); and Michael Hechter, *Principles of Group Solidarity* (Berkeley: University of California Press, 1987).

3. This literature is comparably vast. A synoptic and heroically brief review of it is Calvin Morrill, "Culture and Organization Theory," *Annals of the American Academy of Political and Social Science* 619 (2008):15–40. The quote is from Elisabeth S. Clemens, "Organizational Form as Frame: Collective Identity and Political Strategy in the American Labor Movement, 1880–1920," in Doug McAdam, John D. McCarthy, and Mayer N. Zald (eds.), *Comparative Perspectives on Social Movements: Political Opportunities, Mobilizing Structures, and Cultural Framings* (Cambridge: Cambridge University Press, 1996), pp. 205–226. An elegant effort to bridge the rational choice and culturalist traditions is Micahel Suk-Young Chwe, *Rational Ritual: Culture, Coordination, and Common Knowledge* (Princeton: Princeton University Press, 2003).

4. See Veronica Boix Mansilla, Michèle Lamont, and Kyoko Sato, "Shared Cognitive-Emotional-Interactional Platforms: Markers and Conditions for Interdisciplinary Collaborations." *Science, Technology and Human Values* (November 2015):1–42. For a recent review of team collaboration in science and its effects on participants, see Erin Leahey, "From Sole Investigator to Team Scientist: Trends in the Practice and Study of Research Collaboration," *Annual Review of Sociology* 42 (2016):81–100.

5. Jerry A. Jacobs, *In Defense of Disciplines: Interdisciplinarity and Specialization in the Research University* (Chicago: University of Chicago Press, 2013). On centers and institutes see especially chapter 5.

6. Association is a key mechanism for accruing prestige generally. See Joel M. Podolny, *Status Signals: A Sociological Study of Market Competition* (Princeton: Princeton University Press, 2005).

7. This is not to say that the normative model for a research university is static. As we explained in Chapter 1, the US university is a remarkably flexible form in historical terms. We will revisit the important matter of institutional change in Chapter 6. Our point here is that the current cultural and collective-action templates for making a "real" research university include all the necessary ingredients for stone-soup processes of knowledge production.

8. We borrow these pseudonyms from Amy J. Binder and Kate Wood, *Becoming Right: How Campuses Shape Young Conservatives* (Princeton: Princeton University Press, 2013).

Chapter 5: Numbers and Languages

1. Clark Kerr, *The Uses of the University* (Cambridge, MA: Harvard University Press, 1963).

2. C. P. Snow, *The Two Cultures* (London: Cambridge University Press, 1959).

3. For an early review see Julie Thompson Klein, *Interdisciplinarity: History, Theory, and Practice* (Detroit: Wayne State University Press, 1990).

4. A concise journalistic account of this evolution appears in the second chapter of Kevin Carey's *The End of College* (New York: Riverhead Books, 2015), pp. 14–32. For academic citations see the notes of our account in Chapter 3.

5. Per our discussion in Chapter 3, this way of thinking about disciplinary audiences is based in Andrew Abbott's conceptualization. See Andrew Abbott, *Chaos of Disciplines* (Chicago: University of Chicago Press, 2001); also Andrew Abbott, "Status and Status Strain in the Professions," *American Journal of Sociology* 86 (1981):815–835.

6. For vivid documentation of the reluctant internationalism of US disciplinary social science see Charles Kurzman, "Scholarly Attention and the Limited Internationalization of US Social Science" *International Sociology,* forthcoming. Also Charles Kurzman, "The Stubborn Parochialism of American Social Science," *The Chronicle of Higher Education* (19 January 2015).

7. Michèle Lamont, *How Professors Think: Inside the Curious World of Academic Judgment* (Cambridge, MA: Harvard University Press, 2009); Julie R. Posselt, *Inside Graduate Admissions: Merit, Diversity, and Faculty Gatekeeping* (Cambridge, MA: Harvard University Press, 2016).

8. A definitive historical account of this evolution in the US academic profession is Dorothy Ross, *The Origins of American Social Science* (Cambridge: Cambridge University Press, 1991). See especially chapters 6, 7, and 8 on Economics, Political Science, and Sociology respectively. For germinal statements on professional abstraction see Andrew Abbott, *The*

System of Professions: An Essay on the Division of Expert Labor (Chicago: University of Chicago Press, 1988). Also Andrew Abbott, *Chaos of Disciplines*. On the relationship between the technical structure and epistemology of science generally see Karin Knorr-Cetina, *Epistemic Cultures: How the Sciences Make Knowledge* (Cambridge, MA: Harvard University Press, 1999).

9. The famous metaphor is from Clifford Geertz, "Thick Description: Toward an Interpretive Theory of Culture," in Clifford Geertz, *The Interpretation of Cultures* (New York, Basic Books, 1973), pp. 3–30.

10. Scholarly literature pertaining to this tension is vast. For a concise review see George Steinmetz's introduction "Positivism and Its Others in the Social Sciences," in George Steinmetz, editor, *The Politics of Method in the Human Sciences* (Durham, NC: Duke University Press, 2005), pp. 1–56. Historical sociologists have wrestled with this tension quite directly. See, for example, Elisabeth S. Clemens, "Logics of History? Agency, Multiplicity, and Incoherence in the Explanation of Change," in Julia Adams, Elisabeth S. Clemens, and Ann Shola Orloff (eds.), *Remaking Modernity: Politics, History, and Sociology* (Durham, NC: Duke University Press, 2005), pp. 493–515. Carol A. Heimer carefully specifies the epistemological features of this distinction in "Cases and Biographies: An Essay on Routinization and the Nature of Comparison," *Annual Review of Sociology* 27 (2001):47–76.

11. Critiques of the authenticity of particularistic knowledge include Edward Said's landmark *Orientalism* (New York: Random House, 1978); also James Clifford and George E. Marcus (eds.), *Writing Culture: The Poetics and Politics of Ethnography* (Berkeley: University of California Press, 1986). For examples of critiques of the ontology of generalized knowledge in social science see the essays collected in George Steinmetz (ed.), *The Politics of Method in the Human Sciences* (Durham, NC: Duke University Press, 2005). Also Raewyn Connell, "Northern Theory: The Political Geography of General Social Science," *Theory and Society* 35 (2006):237–264.

12. Jerry A. Jacobs, *In Defense of Disciplines: Interdisciplinarity and Specialization in the Research University* (Chicago: University of Chicago Press, 2013).

13. Daniel Hirschman and Elizabeth Popp Berman, "Do Economists Make Policies? On the Political Effects of Economics." *Socio-Economic Review* 12 (2014):779–811.

14. On the prominence of economists generally see Marion Fourcade, Etienne Ollion, and Yann Algan, "The Superiority of Economists," *Journal of Economic Perspectives* 29 (2015):1–28.

15. David C. Engerman, *Know Your Enemy: The Rise and Fall of America's Soviet Experts* (New York: Oxford University Press, 2009), p. 255.

16. R. A. Palat, "Fragmented Visions: Excavating the Future of Area Studies in a Post-American World," in In M. E. Peters (ed.), *After the Disciplines: the Emergence of Cultural Studies* (Westport, CT: Greenwood Publishing Group, 1999), pp. 64–106. Quote is from p. 77.

17. Wendy Nelson Espeland and Michael Sauder, *Engines of Anxiety: Academic Rankings, Reputation, and Accountability* (New York: Russell Sage Foundation, 2016).

18. For general statements on the preponderance of quantitative modes of valuation in modern societies see Wendy Nelson Espeland and Mitchell L. Stevens, "A Sociology of Quantification," *European Journal of Sociology* XLIX (2008):401–436; also Alain Desrosières, *The Politics of Large Numbers: A History of Statistical Reasoning* (Cambridge, MA: Harvard University Press, 1998).

19. Subsequent to the completion of our fieldwork, the ongoing rise of so-called "big data"—numerical data streams produced through digital media and easily integrated and investigated through advances in computational capacity—suggests an epochal shift in the character of quantitative social science and a further ratcheting up of the analytic skills required to pursue it. The related and rapid development of bibliometrics makes the future of what we here call qualitative analysis newly open as well.

20. There is preponderant evidence of an academic caste system in the disciplinary social sciences, in which top departments tend to hire from a very small number of other top departments. For political science see Robert Oprisko, "Superpowers: The American Academic Elite," *The Georgetown Public Policy Review* (December 3, 2012). For sociology see Val Burris, "The Academic Caste System: Prestige Hierarchies in PhD Exchange Networks," *American Sociological Review* 69 (2004):239–264. Whether or not this system makes for productive scholars is an open question: for economics, see John P. Conley and Ali Sina Onder, "The Research Productivity of New PhDs in Economics: The Surprisingly High Non-success of the Successful." *Journal of Economic Perspectives* 28(2014): 205–216.

21. Posselt is especially thoughtful about this in *Inside Graduate Admissions*.

22. Sharon Coppman, Cindy L. Cain, and Erin Leahy, "The Joy of Science: Disciplinary Diversity in Emotional Accounts." *Science, Technology, & Human Values* 40 (2015):30–70; Anna Neuman, Professing Passion: Emotion in the Scholarship of Professors at Research Universities." *American Educational Research Journal* 43(2006):381–424. For a broad review of scholarship on this basic insight see Michèle Lamont, "Toward a Comparative Sociology of Valuation and Evaluation." *Annual Review of Sociology* 38 (2012):201–221.

Chapter 6: US Universities in the World

1. The Social Science Research Council, a crucial player in the development of post–World War II area studies, dramatically reorganized its international program in 1996—effectively concluding its decades-long incubation of the area studies model. See Zachary Lockman, *Field Notes: The Making of Middle East Studies in the United States* (Stanford, CA: Stanford University Press, 2016), pp. 249–265; also Kenton W. Worcester, *Social*

Science Research Council, 1923–1998 (New York: Social Science Research Council, 2001).

2. Cynthia Miller-Idriss and Elizabeth Hanauer, "Transnational Higher Education: Offshore Campuses in the Middle East," *Comparative Education* 47 (2011):181–207.

3. For a synoptic review of this turbulent period see the essays in Michael W. Kirst and Mitchell L. Stevens, editors, *Remaking College: The Changing Ecology of Higher Education* (Stanford, CA: Stanford University Press, 2015); also the essays in Elizabeth Popp Berman, and Catherine Paradeise, *The University Under Pressure*. Research in the Study of Organizations, Vol. 46 [2016].

4. See Charles Kurzman, "The Stubborn Parochialism of American Social Science," *The Chronicle of Higher Education*, January 19, 2015. Also Charles Kurzman, "Scholarly Attention and the Limited Internationalization of US Social Science," *International Sociology*, forthcoming.

5. Ronald N. Jacobs and Eleanor Townsley, *The Space of Opinion: Media Intellectuals and the Public Sphere* (New York: Oxford University Press, 2011).

6. On the rise of think tanks in the second half of the twentieth century see Thomas Medvetz, *Think Tanks in America* (Chicago: University of Chicago Press, 2012).

7. Christopher Bail, *Terrified: How Anti-Muslim Fringe Organizations Became Mainstream* (Princeton: Princeton University Press, 2015).

8. See Fabio Rojas, *From Black Power to Black Studies: How a Radical Social Movement Became an Academic Discipline* (Baltimore: The Johns Hopkins University Press, 2007). For women's studies, Asian American Studies, and Queer Studies see Michaela Mariel-Lemonik Arthur, *Student Activism and Curricular Change in Higher Education* (Burlington, VT: Ashgate, 2011).

9. American Association of University Professors, *Tenure and Teaching-Intensive Appointments* (2014). www.aaup.org/report/tenure-and-teaching -intensive-appointments, accessed 14 April 2015.

PS CS PRINCETON STUDIES IN CULTURAL SOCIOLOGY

Paul J. DiMaggio, Michèle Lamont,
Robert J. Wuthnow, and Viviana A. Zelizer,
Series Editors

Bearing Witness: Readers, Writers, and the Novel in Nigeria by Wendy Griswold

Gifted Tongues: High School Debate and Adolescent Culture by Gary Alan Fine

Offside: Soccer and American Exceptionalism by Andrei S. Markovits and Steven L. Hellerman

Reinventing Justice: The American Drug Court Movement by James L. Nolan, Jr.

Kingdom of Children: Culture and Controversy in the Homeschooling Movement by Mitchell L. Stevens

Blessed Events: Religion and Home Birth in America by Pamela E. Klassen

Negotiating Identities: States and Immigrants in France and Germany by Riva Kastoryano, translated by Barbara Harshav

Contentious Curricula: Afrocentrism and Creationism in American Public Schools by Amy J. Binder

Community: Pursuing the Dream, Living the Reality by Suzanne Keller

The Minds of Marginalized Black Men: Making Sense of Mobility, Opportunity, and Future Life Chances by Alford A. Young, Jr.

Framing Europe: Attitudes to European Integration in Germany, Spain, and the United Kingdom by Juan Díez Medrano

Interaction Ritual Chains by Randall Collins

On Justification: Economies of Worth by Luc Boltanski and Laurent Thévenot, translated by Catherine Porter

Talking Prices: Symbolic Meanings of Prices on the Market for Contemporary Art by Olav Velthuis

Elusive Togetherness: Church Groups Trying to Bridge America's Divisions by Paul Lichterman

Religion and Family in a Changing Society by Penny Edgell

Hollywood Highbrow: From Entertainment to Art by Shyon Baumann

Partisan Publics: Communication and Contention across Brazilian Youth Activist Networks by Ann Mische

Disrupting Science: Social Movements, American Scientists, and the Politics of the Military, 1945–1975 by Kelly Moore

Weaving Self-Evidence: A Sociology of Logic by Claude Rosental, translated by Catherine Porter